GUIDE TO
ARCHAEOLOGY

D0571624

PAUL BAHN

© Haynes Publishing 2019
First published August 2019

A CIP Catalogue record for this book
is available from the British Library.

ISBN: 978 1 78521 586 5 (print)
ISBN: 978 1 78521 633 6 (eBook)

Library of Congress control no. 2019934677

Published by Haynes Publishing,
Sparkford, Yeovil, Somerset BA22 7JJ
Tel: 01963 440635
Int. tel: +44 1963 440635
Website: www.haynes.com

Printed in Malaysia.

Bluffer's Guide®, Bluffer's® and Bluff Your Way®
are registered trademarks.

Series Editor: David Allsop.

CONTENTS

ß

'Archaeologists are the precise opposite of dustmen, though they often dress like them.'

WHAT IS ARCHAEOLOGY?

If history is bunk, then archaeology is junk. This bizarre subject entails seeking, retrieving and studying the abandoned, lost, broken and discarded traces left by human beings in the past. Archaeologists are therefore the precise opposite of dustmen, though they often dress like them.

Little did ancient peoples* suspect that the garbage they so readily discarded would one day be resurrected by these scientific rag-and-bone merchants. Had they suspected, they might have taken better care of things, and attached some handy labels to explain the objects and what they did with them. As they didn't, archaeologists have to try to figure it all out for themselves.

Archaeology is rather like a vast, fiendish jigsaw puzzle invented by the devil as an instrument of tantalising torment, since:

(*) A seasoned bluffer can gain an important advantage early in any conversation by pouncing fiercely on any use of terms such as 'man, mankind, manmade, early man, fossil man, Neanderthal man, man the hunter', and so forth, as being naively and offensively sexist. This should put your opponent off balance for some time.

a   it will never be finished
b   you don't know how many pieces are missing
c   most of them are lost for ever
d   you can't cheat by looking at the picture.

Prehistoric persons did not always have the foresight to use materials like stone or pottery that survive the ages, and untold quantities of objects have decayed and disappeared. This is bad news for the archaeologist, but wonderful news for you.

Archaeology is an ideal subject in which to become an accomplished bluffer because:

1   Much of the time the evidence is so patchy that anyone's guess is as valid as anyone else's. You can't prove anything. Where the remote past is concerned, nobody knows what took place. The best that can be offered is an informed guess. This you should dress up with the grand title of 'deduction' or 'theory', or (grander still) 'hypothesis'.
2   Though most people profess an interest in the past, if you talk about archaeology with non-archaeologists for more than a few minutes, their eyes tend to glaze over.
3   It is easy to pass yourself off as an expert, full of impressive and esoteric knowledge, since the field is filled with obscure terms and exotic names and places. Even if the general public has heard of them, it is almost certain they will know little or nothing about them. Thus a minimum of homework will go a very long way.

It is therefore child's play to give the false impression of being informed, and few will dare to challenge your facts or your hypotheses. Any inkling that your audience forms part of the huge number of people who, thanks to movies and cartoons, believe that early humans lived alongside dinosaurs, can similarly be used as an opportunity for a derisive snort or a pitying sigh before you enlighten them about the gap of many millions of years between the two life forms.

Never let the fact that nothing is really known about past events stand in your way: instead, use it to your advantage. Some eminent archaeologists have built their entire careers upon convincing bluff.

𝕭

'An archaeologist's career lies in ruins from the start.'

BEING AN ARCHAEOLOGIST

It takes very special qualities to devote one's life to problems with no attainable solutions and to poking around in dead people's garbage: words like 'nosy', 'masochistic' and 'completely crazy' spring readily to mind. This is why eccentricity is a hallmark of the profession. So is an addiction to alcohol (in fact archaeology could be a synonym for alcoholism). You can wryly attribute this fact either to the need to drown one's sorrows in the face of unattainable solutions, or simply to acute embarrassment at practising an inherently ridiculous and often futile profession.

The popular image of archaeologists is that of a bunch of absent-minded scruffs and misfits covered in dust and cobwebs. The bluffer will stress, however, with a knowing smile, that this is not always true – some of them are only slightly absent-minded, and a few keep quite clean.

You can recognise an archetypal archaeologist from the beard, curved pipe, shapeless sweater or T-shirt, and sandals or hiking boots – and that's only the women.

The pipe is usually an affectation, designed to convey the false impression that the archaeologist is a real Sherlock Holmes – a classic prop in bluffing. Beards lend an air of wisdom and maturity, but are basically a means of getting an extra five minutes in bed. The sweaters serve to conceal innumerable figure flaws (most commonly caused by too much beer) while T-shirts unfortunately draw attention to them.

Clothing and footwear depend on temperature, conditions and income, and are often worn for days or weeks without being changed. It is important to pretend to believe that this is caused by remoteness from a water source or laundrette, and is not attributable to a low standard of personal hygiene, or simply sheer lack of interest.

Most archaeologists, if asked why they devote their lives to the subject, will wax lyrical about:

a their passion for the past
b their desire to make a modest contribution to piecing together our picture of human development and history.

Some will even claim that, like Schliemann (see page 104), they have pursued this goal single-mindedly since childhood. Don't believe a word of it: as a good bluffer you should be able to recognise self-serving twaddle at 20 paces. If a group of archaeologists were transported into the past in a time machine, the chances are that they would be thoroughly stupefied within a few hours, and yearning for air conditioning, real ale, and their own version of how things might have been in the past.

THE BENEFITS

In reality most people are attracted to archaeology for a variety of more practical reasons. Here are the main five.

1 To have fun. This is, on occasions, quite possible: it has even been described as the most fun you can have with your pants on.

2 To have an activity/adventure holiday and meet people of the opposite sex. If you get jaded spending your spare time lying on a beach and reading a thriller, and want to get away from package tourists, then some archaeological fieldwork may seem like the ideal solution. Most field directors (the team leader on the ground) insist that you join up for at least a fortnight. This is so that you can't flee in horror when you discover that you are just unpaid labour and trapped in a group of equally tiresome people, many of whom take the work extremely seriously.

'Archaeology is a beautiful mistress but she brings a poor dowry'

Jean-François Champollion

---

3 To read for a university degree in a subject that is generally regarded as cushier than most. At the end of it, some students decide to go on to do a Ph.D., either because they can think of nothing better to do, or because they can't face entering the real world and

finding a proper job. As it is, many drop out along the way. Of those that get their Ph.D., most find there are no jobs in archaeology, they have wasted several years, and that all that remains is to retrain as an accountant or tax inspector. Here their passion for the past quickly withers, to be replaced by mammon and middle age.

4 To make a living (not recommended unless your material needs are minimal). As Champollion (see page 58) said, archaeology is a beautiful mistress but she brings a poor dowry.

5 To make a career. This is not easy, for an archaeologist's career lies in ruins from the start.

An archaeological career is considered successful if the archaeologist becomes:

– a national celebrity (rare)
– an international celebrity (very rare), or
– wealthy (extremely rare – 'wealth' and 'archaeological career' are almost contradictions in terms).

This is usually done by making an important discovery with public appeal. Virtually all professional archaeologists today stress that they are not treasure-hunters but scientists, seeking information rather than objects. Therefore, in any conversation that focuses on individual treasures, the bluffer can score points by emphasising, with great condescension, that nowadays archaeologists dig not to find things but to find things out.

This is generally true, but it is also fair to say that

any archaeologist would be overjoyed to find something that not only proved important to the subject but which also caught the public imagination. And since very few discoveries, if presented soberly, would rouse more than a stifled yawn from the average television viewer or tabloid reader, they have to be dressed up with bluffers' superlatives: the first, the oldest, the biggest, the best-preserved, richest, most spectacular of their kind.

Another effective ploy is to associate the find with a perennially popular topic such as:

– sex
– gore
– cannibalism.

Remember, too, that since the public cares little for anonymous ancestors, it is crucial to link the find to a well-known historical or legendary figure, preferably royal: King Arthur is a firm favourite, but Leicester archaeologists really hit the jackpot in a municipal car park in 2012 by unearthing human remains that seemed to be those of Richard III, a truly famous monarch – this was worldwide news, and led to a whole string of TV documentaries and books. The discovery of the umpteenth Roman skeleton or Egyptian mummy will arouse no interest, but if you present them as possibly Julius Caesar's grandmother, or Queen Nefertiti, you will hit the headlines and perhaps even the talk shows. Your colleagues may sneer but will be green with envy when they see the exposure and increased funding that this sort of thing will get you.

As a bluffer, you should pour scorn on all such attention-seeking as 'tub-thumping by unscrupulous and ambitious careerists'. If accused of it yourself you should explain that, sadly, this kind of thing is a necessary evil to keep archaeology in the public eye, and that you allowed your work to be distorted by the media only with the greatest reluctance and with no thought of furthering your career.

TYPES OF BLUFFER

It will come as no surprise therefore to discover that anyone who takes up archaeology as a profession is, or has to become, a consummate bluffer:

Students are novice bluffers, trying to learn the rudiments of the subject in order to bluff their way through examinations and into a career or, at least, a degree. This entails a certain amount of reading and writing, but also some participation in mundane fieldwork in order to gain experience and ingratiate themselves with their teachers.

Lecturers usually have a large teaching workload and cannot therefore be expected to think and be original as well. They are practised bluffers through having to convince their audience that they know lots of things outside their particular field of interest, and have not swotted it all up the night before. Unlike lecturers in most other subjects, their real work starts in the summer vacation when they may do a bit of research, or direct some fieldwork, or try to make some headway with the book they've been meaning to write for years. Their main goal is to get a better salary and a reduced workload by becoming:

Senior Academics. These are advanced bluffers. Once these dizzy heights have been reached, it is possible to sit back and rest on your laurels: for example, one archaeological head-of-department in England did absolutely nothing for 40 years after the appearance of a thesis, and was therefore nicknamed 'Thrombosis', the clot that blocks up the system. Another just wrote prefaces to books of other people's work. Others tread water by constantly producing variations on the same piece of work. One or two manage to remain fresh and inventive, and produce interesting work, but they are exceptions and out of place in a book on bluffing.

Note that none of these more advanced positions will give an ounce of glory to the department **Secretaries**, who are the most important people in academic archaeology as they are usually the sanest individuals in the subject. They do all the hard work, and without them most academics and departments would simply fall apart.

Dinosaurs. This category denotes those elderly archaeologists who are long retired, but refuse to make a dignified exit, or to give way to younger, up-and-coming colleagues – for some reason, this is quite prevalent in France. Instead they cling on to their power and influence, hogging the limelight, and often do their best to prevent the younger generation from replacing them, let alone disproving their pet theories. In this regard, the accomplished bluffer could quote the Roman emperor Marcus Aurelius, who suggested that there is a decent time to make an exit from public life instead of sticking around long after the appropriate moment.

'Professional archaeologists need to take a vow of poverty, though not, fortunately, one of chastity.'

The dinosaurs apparently imagine that they are loved for themselves, so they feel impelled to carry on out of a duty to their public. This egotism and altruism are fatally compounded, giving off a gas which corrodes their reputation as fast as it goes to their head, while the critical onlooker falls unconscious....

Professional archaeologists need to take a vow of poverty, though not, fortunately, one of chastity. Most of them choose to substitute interest or leisure for income. Being slender of means (though broad of belly), they constantly have to apply and beg for grants:

a) to do fieldwork
b) to attend conferences
c) to get things published.

You should know that these applications never tell the truth about the low degree of importance or originality in the project, but rather stress the potentially crucial and fascinating nature of the work.

A FEW TRUTHS

It is sad but true to say that:

* The only way to make good money from archaeology is to bluff your way to becoming a professor (although this is now a somewhat debased currency, in Britain at least, since practically everyone is now given this title which used to be limited to the head of department).
* The only way to make excellent money is to get on TV, talk with breathless enthusiasm, and bluff the public into thinking you are an expert on the subject.
* The only way to make vast amounts of money from it is to write *The Clan of the Cave Bear*.

𝕭

'As bluffers know better than anyone, a university degree does not necessarily provide any indication of intelligence, creativity, imagination, dedication, originality or competence.'

TYPES OF ARCHAEOLOGIST

'AMATEURS' AND 'PROFESSIONALS'

The past belongs to everybody, and nobody has a monopoly on knowledge about archaeology. Yet from the subject's earliest days, elitism, snobbery, closed shops and exclusivity have been constantly evident among archaeologists. In other words, 'professionals' and 'amateurs' have often been uneasy bedfellows. As bluffers know better than anyone, a university degree does not necessarily provide any indication of intelligence, creativity, imagination, dedication, originality or competence, as can be seen in countless examples all around us. Yet many 'professionals' believe such a degree bestows some divine right to consider themselves above the hoi polloi. Some take this to such extremes that they feel the need to pretend they have an even higher degree than they actually possess. Accordingly many archaeologists, especially in the past, have treated 'amateurs' or 'avocational scholars' as somehow second-class citizens.

Some of the most unethical behaviour, some of the silliest theories and some of the worst misuses of data in recent years have come out of 'professionals'. Of course, 'amateurs' include many eccentrics, and they come up with a lot of off-beat theories; but it's really the pot calling the kettle black: archaeology is absolutely stuffed with eccentrics, people who hoard data, people who don't publish. The 'professionals' have developed a system of cliques; they've got their in-groups and their out-groups, they've got their rat-race, and they've got their mutual admiration societies, their back-stabbing and their infighting, all of which can be summed up as 'You play ball with me and I'll scratch yours.' Some of the academics seem to think they can walk on water, they seem to think they're infallible, and they gather together a bunch of disciples or followers around them, generally known as 'mafias'.

Bluffers can point out that 'amateurs' often know far more than 'professionals', and that they have always been the backbone and the strength of archaeology – in the early days they were often clerics, medics, lawyers and schoolteachers. As the term 'amateur' itself indicates, they really love their subject. Countless important sites have been discovered by 'amateurs', and many sites have been well excavated by them.

Yet each group has often tended to view the other with suspicion, scorn or even contempt. In some parts of the world in recent years there has been an unfortunate tendency to make archaeology more 'professional' by gradually edging out the 'amateurs', so that enthusiastic volunteers may now find it very difficult to take part in digs. Owing to the increasing commercialisation of the subject, many clients insist that the workforce must be entirely 'professional' and insurance policies often exclude or make very difficult the use of volunteers. However, the traditional system still exists in some regions such as eastern Europe, where numerous unskilled labourers can be employed, supervised by a small number of 'professional' archaeologists.

Be that as it may, there are two basic categories of archaeologist: the Field Archaeologist and the Armchair Archaeologist.

FIELD ARCHAEOLOGISTS

Often called 'Dirt Archaeologists', a term that may not necessarily apply to their minds or their appearance, though it often does, they are the ones who actually go out and dig or survey in order to obtain some evidence to investigate. They are also the ones who try to live up to the Indiana Jones 'Action Man' image, usually with a marked lack of success.

Field Archaeologists can generally bluff an audience into believing their work is exciting and full of thrills; but you should know that, just like the world of movie-making or fashion photography, while it may look glamorous and enviable from the outside, if you try it you soon discover the long periods of nothing much happening.

There are compensations, of course: few other occupations enable you to go off into the wilds at regular intervals with a bunch of nubile youngsters who are eager to have fun and obtain good grades. This is why many long-suffering non-archaeological spouses feel obliged to go along too.

Field Archaeologists tend to get sunburn, insect bites, blistered hands/knees/feet, frequent hangovers, and the runs.

ARMCHAIR ARCHAEOLOGISTS

Armchair archaeologists, also known as shiny bums, choose their role for a variety of reasons: idleness, incompetence, an unwillingness to dirty their hands, or an aversion to sunlight.

They sustain the traditional image of archaeologists as dreary old fogies or, in many cases, young fogies. As they cannot or will not obtain evidence of their own, they have to turn to other people's. Nevertheless they can achieve real eminence in the subject by practising a special kind of bluffing known as 'Theoretical Archaeology'. This is done by:

1 Concealing a lack of data by questioning the validity of everyone else's:
   – How well was the site dug?
   – How representative was the sample?
2 Deflecting attention from a lack of ideas and solutions by attacking those trying to do some work and by trying to demolish their whole approach to the subject.

This intimidation and sermonising once paid amazing dividends in many careers, particularly within what was called the 'New Archaeology' of the 1970s and 1980s. If its practitioners were sufficiently loud, rude and aggressive, generations of students came to treat them with extraordinary respect and deference. This was known as the 'Alpha Baboon Syndrome', since monkeys achieve dominance with the same kind of blustering bluff.

But behaviour alone is not sufficient: it is necessary to say or print something. Theoretical archaeologists (or 'the Living Dead', as they are known) put out enormous quantities of papers and books, filled with:

a impressive jargon
b long words
c mathematical equations
d complicated diagrams involving a mass of lines, arrows and boxes.

Few people ever read this stuff apart from other theoreticians trying to keep up with new jargon (and looking for something new to attack), and those students unfortunate enough to have the authors among their teachers. Consequently, very few people ever realise that much of the text is meaningless, the equations pointless, and the diagrams superfluous, so the industry keeps on rolling along. Here is a genuine example of a sentence from a theoretical work:

'The notion of structural contradictions resulting in societal change relates to the operation of causative variables at a different epistemological level from that assumed in analysis of interlinked variables and entities resulting in morphogenic feedback processes.'

Despite its apparent sophistication, this kind of hoodwinking is remarkably easy: just learn a few key words like 'cognitive', 'operationalise' and 'interpretive' (not interpretative – this is primarily an American skill); then string them together with appropriate jargon like 'structuralist', 'processual' or even 'post-processual' (don't worry about what they mean – nobody else knows or cares), and you can waffle happily until your audience or readers doze off.

If you are ever confronted by a frightening number of theoretical archaeologists (two), you should first try to talk positively about the merits of fieldwork. If they persist, try quoting Kant's dictum that 'concepts without percepts are empty' (i.e. you can't get a grasp of the whole without delving into some minutiae, in other words, get on and do some real work). Criticism by a real German philosopher should strike to their very heart, or at least stun them long enough for you to make your excuses and your escape.

Armchair Archaeologists tend to get ego mania, permanent hangovers and ulcers.

The difference can be summed up very simply: Field Archaeologists dig rubbish up, Theoretical Archaeologists write it down.

LAB RATS AND GEEKS

There are now a substantial number of 'scientific archaeologists', based in laboratories, who delve into everything – the organic traces of environmental archaeology, analyses of metal and stone, conservation, dating, and so forth. Thanks to the incredible surge in computer applications in every aspect of archaeology, we are surrounded by nerds and geeks who spend their lives crunching data, in the hope of identifying some meaningful patterns. And the subject is now drowning in (or enjoying, depending on your point of view) an ocean of archaeology websites, online databases, online research facilities, etc. Some aspects of this revolution are very positive – e.g. the new accessibility through the web of many doctoral theses and old journals and publications. Unfortunately, this also means that many old-fashioned libraries are being put out of business. Some university libraries now contain almost no books, only computer screens!

These desk-bound lost souls are the people who look after the records of previous archaeological discoveries and investigations – so they are record-holders, but not the kind that make it into the *Guinness Book of Records*. They constitute a public repository for information about archaeological sites, and also provide a public information service about anything to do with 'Heritage' or 'the Historic Environment', to use current jargon. In addition, they can offer advice – sometimes solicited, sometimes unwelcome – to landowners about the management of any archaeological sites or landscapes on their property. They also offer their invaluable insights to planners and developers about the possible archaeological implications of what they want to do – their 'development proposals' – and they monitor the quality of any archaeological fieldwork carried out in response to these plans. In this area of their work, they often come into contact with:

CONSULTANTS

Otherwise known as parasites and hangers-on, these characters have sprung up since 1990, and their main purpose seems to be to muddy the waters and cream off a slice of archaeology's meagre funding. A bluffer might venture the opinion that it is hard to see the point of them beyond the understandable ambition of upholding their lifestyles. What they are supposed to do is offer independent advice to their clients – usually developers or companies who are obliged by law to check out the land they want to build on to see if there are any inconvenient and irritating archaeological remains in the way of progress. (It is worth noting, however, that with typical hypocrisy British government building projects were exempt from this law until recently, and so they could completely ignore sites of archaeological interest and build whatever they wanted wherever they liked.) In practice, however, many consultants appear to be more intent on protecting their clients' interests than being concerned about archaeology. They know only too well on which side their bread is buttered and where it comes from…

ARCHAEOLOGY IN THE FIELD

At some point in their careers, most archaeologists, with the exception of theoreticians, actually go outside and try to obtain some fresh information.

FINDING SITES

The simplest way to find sites is to ask somebody who knows where they are. The smart bluffer should be aware that the most important sites are not found by archaeologists at all – instead they are found accidentally by farmers, quarrymen, construction workers, from aerial photographs or geophysical survey; underwater sites are discovered by fishermen and divers; caves have been found by pot-holers, children, even dogs (in the case of Lascaux & Altamira). In fact, professional tomb-robbers are far more adept at finding ancient graves than any archaeologists. However, it is the latter who investigate the sites and who get all the publicity and the kudos.

The particular area where they choose to work is supposedly selected in order to answer questions of specific relevance to their research interest. In practice the real reasons involve some or all of the following factors:

– the climate
– the presence of a lover
– swimming facilities
– the local booze.

For these reasons France is particularly popular. It also offers superb food and a sensible French tendency to put roofs over their excavations.

Another important factor is the political situation: warfare is not a healthy background for archaeological fieldwork. This is why most American archaeologists left Iran when the Ayatollah came to power. Unfortunately, some chose to move to the short-lived safety of Afghanistan. Currently, it would be a brave or suicidal archaeologist who attempted to do fieldwork in that country, or Iraq, or Syria, or Libya, etc…

Whatever the area, there are two principal ways to get new information: excavation and survey.

EXCAVATION

People tend to think that archaeologists spend all their time digging. In fact, not all of them dig, and only a few dig all the time. The bluffer should explain condescendingly that processing and analysing the finds usually take far longer than the excavation itself, which is therefore just the foreplay, the preliminary stage: the means to an end, not an end in itself.

'Excavation tells you a lot about a small area, survey tells you a little about a big one.'

Any excavation that the public can reach is likely to be visited with annoying frequency by honest citizens who think it is there for their amusement. They should be treated with the greatest courtesy and respect in case:

a   they may wish to contribute financially to the project, or,

b   they are connected to someone important who might be able to shut down the work.

Depending on their opinion of the visitors, directors may assign the most charming or the most obnoxious digger to the task of giving guided tours. Directors will usually take on this chore themselves only for VIPs or the media.

Visitors generally offer a limited range of questions and comments, and bluffers should familiarise themselves with the most irritating in order to prepare witty responses worthy of Oscar Wilde or Groucho Marx:

- Found any gold, then?
- Keep going, you might reach Australia, harhar.
- How old is that? How do you know?
- Why did people live in holes in the ground?
- Lost a contact lens, have you?
- Is that a dinosaur bone?
- Would you like to come and dig my garden when you've finished?
- Where's your hat and whip, Indiana?
- What do you do when it rains?
- I think the *Time Team*'s really terrific, don't you?

It has been said that there is no standard or correct way to dig a site, but plenty of wrong ways. This is a useful tip for the bluffer in charge of such a project. You can dismiss any criticism of method as being inapplicable to the particular and unique circumstances present at the site. In fact, there are two basic ways to dig:

1 **Vertically** (to see the different layers)
2 **Horizontally** (to expose wider areas of a particular layer).

Most excavation directors keep their strategies flexible to take advantage of any special features they may encounter, or to camouflage any mistakes that may be made. So you should know that rather than being carefully planned from the start, most digs muddle along by trowel and error.

It is advisable, however, to get as much information as you can about what lies beneath the surface before you start digging. This helps to avoid the embarrassment of:

a finding far more than you were prepared for
b not finding anything
c finding you're digging in the wrong place.

So a whole range of sophisticated techniques and gadgets can be unleashed – the 'geophizz' so beloved of the long-running archaeological TV series *Time Team* – which allow boffins or the more technically minded students to produce vague maps of what is under the soil. These glorified metal-detectors include magnetometers, measurers of soil resistivity, and sundry other ways of passing energy through the ground. If funds do not run to this, probes can be pushed into the ground at frequent intervals. Failure to check out a site adequately led one British archaeologist to dig his way down into the London Underground.

On any dig there are a number of standard characters you will encounter:

The Excavation Director is rather like a general. He (it is most often a he) plans the overall strategy but leaves all the hard work to the infantry, dealing only with the paperwork: supplies, accounts, permits, begging letters, and so forth.

The Site Supervisors or **officers** – often graduate students – act as liaisons between the general and the infantry, and generally make the most of their lofty status. They occasionally have some idea of what is being done at the site and why.

The Diggers or **infantry** – undergraduates, local convicts or civilian volunteers – are the cannon fodder, usually providing all the sweaty labour and kept in a state of blissful ignorance about what they are doing and why. Amazingly, some even pay money to be treated this way, though these days most diggers are paid archaeologists. Their basic task often appears to be to move dirt from one place to another, occasionally sieving it into different sizes before dumping it.

Bluffers should know that much of the time little real digging occurs: the dirt is loosened with a trowel and brushed aside, which is a good deal slower. In most parts of the world the shifting is done with shovels, buckets and wheelbarrows. In Japan, however, where mechanisation is rampant, even minor archaeological sites have the dirt removed on a series of overlapping conveyor belts to the spoilheap.

Other exciting chores include washing the finds (mostly bits of stone, bone or pot), writing tiny numbers on them, and drawing, bagging and cataloguing them. In the past all the information was collected in excavation notebooks, together with exact measurements of the objects' precise position in the site. It did not matter too much if the notebooks were accurate or not – comforting news for the digging bluffer – as there are few things more mind-numbing than trying to make sense of someone else's excavation notes, and the books were usually never looked at again. Today, on most digs, these data are tapped or scanned directly into computers, tablets and other such gizmos which not only means that the machines produce all the site plans far more easily and quickly than students, but also that the more irrelevant and useless data can be ignored even more rapidly than before.

Use of computers, of course, also makes the dig appear to be at the very forefront of modern technology – never mind that they are only as useful and accurate as the information keyed into them in the first place, which in turn depends on the quality and vigilance of the excavators as well as of the computer operators. Computer printouts, maps, diagrams and 3D reconstructions make your reports look terrifically impressive and professional, and have the extra advantage that they usually deter readers from examining your evidence very closely.

Some directors, probably those who had a deservedly lonely childhood, object to diggers chatting as they work. This makes an already dull job unbearable. Faced with days of unremittingly tedious labour of this kind, it is little wonder that most diggers secretly long to make an exciting find, a body perhaps or even some treasure. This is not advisable, however, as it can lead to visits by looters, or complaints and threats from local people who object to their ancestors being disturbed, and of course there is the ever-present possibility of curses (see page 65).

Diggers need strong knees in order to cope with long hours working bent-legged on planks or subsoils: being a Catholic or Japanese is useful training here.

Sites can generally be divided into two types:

1 **Wetland** (full of soggy wood)
2 **Dryland** (no soggy wood at all).

Wetland archaeologists have a superiority complex as they are able to find the kind of perishable stuff that has normally disintegrated on dryland sites. They risk developing trench-foot. Dryland archaeologists have a far less messy time of it, and only risk pneumoconiosis (the lung disease caused by inhalation of dust) but only if the site is really dry.

Work on either kind of site should help you build up muscles, lose weight (not in France), and get a tan – though not in Britain. This is partly due to the weather but also because many commercial clients enforce strict Health & Safety regimes. In order to avoid the risk of being sued for causing skin cancer, they force all employees to wear neck-to-toe high-viz overalls, and failure to wear them can lead to instant dismissal.

Some people hope that a dig will be like a Club 18–30 holiday, and many are; but there is usually a ranking system in operation, with the most attractive diggers aiming for the director first, the supervisors next, and fellow diggers only as a last resort. One or two French directors in the past were notorious for attracting American 'groupies' to their digs.

Never admit to someone of higher rank that this is your first dig, or that you don't know what you are doing. Apart from being as potentially embarrassing as confessing to virginity, such an admission will lead to your being given all the most menial tasks which practised hands try to avoid, such as making the coffee, digging latrines, or both.

Your equipment and clothes should give the appearance of being well used, and you should assume an air of feigned self-confidence and casualness about the whole business.

FUNDAMENTAL LAWS

There are a few fundamental laws in archaeological excavation with which you should be familiar:

1 The most interesting part of the site will be under your spoilheap (or 'backdirt'), or at least outside the area you choose to dig.
2 The most important find will turn up on the last day or when you're pressed for time and funds (this is known as the Howard Carter law – the famous archaeologist found Tutankhamun just before his funding was to be cut off by Lord Carnarvon).
3 Finding anything worthwhile will involve extending your dig and, in any case, it will not be what you were looking for.
4 If in doubt, hack it out.
5 Only falsify your data where absolutely necessary: this is for the most cynical bluffers who take confidence from the knowledge that every site is unique, excavation destroys it, and so nobody can ever redo your work and prove you wrong.
6 Painted potsherds (broken pieces of ceramic) are always found face-down, like when you drop buttered toast.
7 The number of potsherds rises the longer you sit on the box they're stored in.
8 The number of metates (big grindstones) recovered at the site depends on the distance to the vehicle.

USEFUL THINGS TO TAKE ON AN EXCAVATION:

– Camping equipment.
– Scruffy old clothing, including T-shirt marked 'Archaeologists do it in holes'.
– A pointing trowel (in France a bent screwdriver is preferred, which tells you something about the French). Make sure it looks old and battered enough to pass yourself off as a veteran.
– Insurance (in case a trench collapses on you).
– A bottle opener and corkscrew.
– Condoms.
– Insect repellent (especially crucial when relieving oneself in a cloud of Siberian mosquitoes).

SURVEY

The principal 'active' alternative to excavation these days is surface survey. This involves systematically walking a site or landscape, scanning it for archaeological traces of all kinds – walls, structures, bits of stone or pottery, etc. These are then carefully plotted on maps, and information conjured up from the patterns. Survey fans are fiercely proud of their type of work, being conscious of the fact that excavators consider survey a poor relation, and that excavation is the only way to be sure what lies beneath the surface. In fact each method has different strengths: excavation tells you a lot about a small area, survey tells you a little about a big one.

Survey is pretty good for bluffing, because objects are often not even collected, but simply have their presence and location noted. So every survey is unique and can never be repeated exactly. Consequently, nobody can check your facts, and the only way to challenge your claims is to excavate the whole area of your survey.

Survey used to be considered a second-best, undertaken where permission, funds or personnel for a dig were not available. But today it has been realised that survey is faster and a lot less expensive than digging, certainly less destructive, and requires virtually no equipment other than maps, students and stout footwear.

USEFUL THINGS TO TAKE ON A SURVEY:
- Camping equipment.
- Scruffy old clothing, including T-shirt marked 'Archaeologists do it systematically all over the landscape'.
- Floppy hat (if abroad; an umbrella if in Britain).
- Foot powder.
- A compass.
- Sting relief.
- Local phrase book (to check for 'Beware of the bull', 'Electrified fence', 'Minefield', etc.).

CONTRACT ARCHAEOLOGY

Some people are professional diggers, attached to private firms, companies or trusts. Most of their work involves rapid excavation of sites that are threatened with imminent destruction by various causes, particularly development projects. It therefore entails little overall strategy: the stuff is dug up for the sake of it, to preserve it for posterity. Their colleagues in academia who claim to do planned research excavations often scoff at this kind of catch-all procedure. Naturally you should praise Contract Archaeology if faced with a researcher, and vice versa.

THE SPECIALISTS

Something has to be done with all the data gathered in the field, and this is where a wide range of people, many of them outside archaeology itself, are called upon to do their stuff.

STONE TOOL EXPERTS

These individuals are responsible for putting bits of worked stone into different categories according to shape and style, and trying to figure out what they were used for. This has become a little easier in recent decades by looking at wear patterns and residues on their working edges through powerful microscopes: human blood has even been detected on some prehistoric stone tools, which suggests that some makers were as clumsy as modern experimenters. Try to avoid bad jokes about 'chips off the old block', or living on a diet of core 'n' flakes.

Few specialists are less invigorating than those who have devoted their lives to bits of stone, but they are run a close second by:

POTTERY EXPERTS

It may take a crackpot to love a cracked pot, but bits of pottery (or 'sherds' or 'shards') are almost as numerous and as indestructible as stone tools in archaeology, so it is lucky that some people choose this line of work. Trying to reconstruct shattered pots is a frustrating and delicate task, like a 3-D jigsaw, especially if there is a piece missing or several left over. Those who do not wish to be thrown by making a slip need to have an even temper.

ZOOLOGISTS

Archaeologists often depend on zoologists to identify the animal remains they exhume. Bone experts have things easier than their botanical colleagues (see below), as bone fragments are bigger, better preserved and more readily identifiable than plant remains. Hence a growing number of archaeologists feel able to tackle this job, calling themselves 'zoo-archaeologists' or 'archaeozoologists'. The bluffer will, of course, prefer the alternative version to that used.

Some even specialise further, in fish bones, or bird bones, or rodents, or in mollusc shells: snails are a particularly easy subject to keep up with.

BOTANISTS

Archaeologists rely on botanists to identify any bits of vegetation they may dig up (wood, seeds, nuts, grains), no matter how soggy or charred these may be. The botanists often extract the material in a gunge, after putting sediment from the site through a flotation machine or a wet sieve. They then have to peer down microscopes at this ancient muesli and do their best to make sense of it.

Things are a little more interesting if the mixture comes from a stomach. Tollund Man, the preserved Iron Age body of 2100 BP (see Glossary), which was found in a Danish peat bog with a noose round his neck, had a number of plant remains in his stomach, indicating that his last meal was a kind of gruel comprising seeds and grains. On eating a reconstruction of this tasteless mush on TV, Sir Mortimer Wheeler (see page 108) announced that Tollund Man had probably committed suicide if that was the sort of cooking he got at home.

'The study of pollen is, however, a very taxing discipline, and one that gets right up some people's noses.'

Some botanists specialise in the study of pollen (the accomplished bluffer will refer to them as palynologists). Pollen grains survive amazingly well, and can reveal a great deal about past vegetation and climate by showing what was growing in different places and periods. The study of pollen is, however, a very taxing discipline, and one that gets right up some people's noses.

COPROLITE ANALYSTS

Coprolites are ancient faeces, and specimens from animals and humans may be found in archaeological sites, especially very dry ones or waterlogged ones. They represent the most direct evidence for what was actually eaten, so unfortunately their contents need to be extracted and identified. A small number of intrepid experts around the world know how to treat the coprolites with chemicals so that they regain their original form, texture and even their smell.

One American specialist is said to be capable of recognising some substances in treated coprolites (such as liquorice) from the odour alone. These experts are generally and undeservedly given a wide berth by other scholars, since their work comprises such close encounters of the turd kind.

FORENSIC ANTHROPOLOGISTS

When possible human remains are encountered and excavated by archaeologists (or indeed by the public or police), 'forensic anthropologists' are usually brought in to examine them. The more ancient remains are usually dealt with by 'osteologists' or 'palaeo-pathologists'. If these specialists can establish that the remains are indeed human, then they need to set up a biological profile – i.e. figure out the age, sex, stature, and ancestry of the deceased. They might also investigate the time since death, state of health during life, cause of death (evidence of illness or trauma), and sometimes even family resemblances. Developments in biochemistry and genetics are now allowing much more work to be done at the molecular level, although the osteology – the study of bones – remains fundamental. This kind of work can be very stressful – especially where recent murder victims are concerned, let alone mass burials as encountered in Rwanda or the former Yugoslavia – and the specialists may need a few stiff ones when dealing with stiffs.

— *ß* —

'(The tower of Babel's) construction led to disaster, which proves that ziggurats are bad for your health.'

FIELDS OF SPECIALISATION

There is a wide range of interesting sub-disciplines within archaeology on which one can choose to concentrate. A bluffer need only be an 'expert' in whichever subject the other person knows nothing about.

EGYPTOLOGY

Not the liveliest branch of the subject (it is, after all, characterised by the Book of the Dead), this field nevertheless remains popular with the public because of its impressive and photogenic monuments, its mysteries, picture-writing, strange gods and spectacular treasures. Most movies with an archaeological theme are set in Egypt, and usually involve mummies and curses. So if you want to bluff your way in archaeology you clearly need to know a bit about this civilisation.

It is simple to bluff in Egyptology as most non-archaeologists have heard of only a handful of people (Tutankhamun, Cleopatra, and perhaps Cheops and Nefertiti) and sites (Valley of the Kings, the Pyramids,

Abu Simbel), so you can dazzle them without much difficulty by mentioning a couple of obscure pharaohs such as Sesostris or Sheshonk. Should you be faced with someone who has been on a tour of Egypt, you do not need to show any expertise at all, just let them ramble on at length about their experiences and impressions.

In order to demonstrate an intimate knowledge of the less familiar aspects of ancient Egyptian life, you could mention the (absolutely genuine) British Museum papyrus that provides the recipe for a love potion to win a woman's love: the man has to mix some dandruff from a murdered person's scalp with some barley grains and apple pips, then add a little of his own blood and semen, and finally the blood of a tick from a black dog. This mixture, if slipped into the woman's drink, should have devastating consequences. Another winning formula, designed to make a woman enjoy love-making, was to rub the foam from a stallion's mouth into one's own 'obelisk'.

If challenged to translate some hieroglyphics, make up something dull and religious that sounds plausible, and your audience will be satisfied: for example 'O Lord of the Two Kingdoms, Beloved of Nut, the Divine Mother, and of Re, thy enemies prostrate themselves before thy all-conquering chariot.' Another particularly effective bluff is to talk in terms of dynasties – 'that probably dates to the early 13th dynasty' – since everyone will be impressed and nobody will dare to admit they don't know what you're talking about. Even most non-Egyptological archaeologists won't have a clue about fitting dates (much less pharaohs) to dynasties.

Tutankhamun, incidentally, was of the 18th dynasty, Sesostris the 12th, and Sheshonk the 22nd.

THE NEAR EAST

Exactly the same applies to Near Eastern archaeology, since only specialists can remember the difference between Sumerians, Babylonians, Akkadians, Assyrians, Hittites and sundry others. The merest reference to the 3rd dynasty of Ur should establish the depth of your knowledge, while a mention of (King) Nabonidus (see page 103) will confirm your expertise.

The only features of Near Eastern archaeology that you need be familiar with are the royal tombs of Ur with their gold treasures; the great mound-sites known as 'tells'; and the enormous stepped towers called ziggurats (meaning mountain peaks). The most famous of these was the tower of Babel (Babylon): its construction, according to the Bible, led to disaster, which proves that ziggurats are bad for your health.

Bluffers should also be aware that the Dead Sea Scrolls comprise thousands of fragments of ancient Hebrew books, about 2,000 years old, that were found by shepherds tossing a stone into a cave near the Dead Sea in the late 1940s, and that as word spread about the importance of the finds they were able to sell them by the square inch.

The accomplished bluffer will take care to differentiate serious Biblical archaeologists, who investigate sites in the Bible lands, from the fanatics who take the Bible as Gospel and keep trying to find bits of Noah's Ark on Mount Ararat.

ROCK ART

One of the jollier aspects of archaeology, this entails the location, recording and study of ancient carvings and paintings on rocks. Those involved need to be tough (much of the art is in deep caves, high mountains or very hot areas) and include many of the most eccentric characters one could wish to meet.

In recent years there was a vogue in rock art studies for theories involving 'shamans', 'trance', drugs and 'altered states of consciousness'. The line for the bluffer to take is that the media and many gullible readers seem to be 'trance-fixed' by these topics which tell us rather more about obsessed 'shamaniacs' than about the rock art or its creators. But if you want to add to the general myth-making there's not much to prevent you. In the absence of the original artists it is impossible to know very much about these pictures, so this is an ideal area for invention and bluffing.

Better still, many places are almost inaccessible: for example, caves tend to contain sharp stalactites, crevasses, deep water, guano, mosquitoes, and even, in some parts of the world, killer bees. One cave in the Dordogne, mercifully not open to the public, lies beneath the fortified hill town of Domme and has always served as its sewer. The entrance is through a coal bunker in someone's back yard, the cave stinks, and it is wise not to examine too closely the sticky goo that has to be negotiated. Occasionally, during the visit, another load is flushed into the cave from a house above. The purpose of the exercise is to see a single, mediocre Ice

Age drawing of a bison. Few specialists return for a second viewing.

UNDERWATER ARCHAEOLOGY

Excavating on land is hard enough, but some people like to make things extra tricky for themselves, and working underwater is the archaeological equivalent of standing up in a hammock. Bluffers can point out with wry amusement that the best-known practitioner is aptly named George Bass.

'The *Mary Rose* sank only a short distance from port, which does not say much for British shipbuilding even in those days.'

Most of the work is done on the seabed, in harbours, or in lakes, but occasionally it can also involve unusual sites such as the great 'cenote' or sacred well of the Maya in Mexico's Chichén Itzá into which great quantities of gold and jade objects, and (female) virgins according to Spanish accounts, were thrown as sacrifices. You may safely claim that the latter cannot be correct since work by divers and dredgers in the 40 feet of water and 10 feet of muck at the bottom has shown that many of the skeletal remains belong to men and children.

Underwater archaeologists get very excited about

ship designs and cargoes, topics that leave terrestrial colleagues fairly cold unless they find something particularly old or unusual or well preserved. The landlubbers probably harbour a grudge because they cannot see all these sites for themselves except on film. So occasionally the underwater archaeologists raise an entire ship to the surface and finish the study there. This was done with the collection of sodden timbers that used to be the Tudor ship *Mary Rose*.

The *Mary Rose* sank only a short distance from port, which does not say much for British shipbuilding even in those days, and bluffers can stress the fact that archaeological evidence suggests the crew had already started playing dice before the voyage was properly underway, which might be seen as the 16th-century equivalent of leaving the bow doors open.

URBAN ARCHAEOLOGY

Much work has been done on archaeological sites within towns and cities in recent decades, partly through a growing interest in the urban past, but more often through sheer necessity as more and more demolition and construction go on, giving archaeologists a brief chance between operations to look at what lies under the chosen site. If you find brick foundations, soggy leather shoes, glazed potsherds, clay pipes and endless quantities of chicken bones a source of great fascination, then this is the field for you. Occasionally the town may stretch back beyond the medieval period, and then you can also delve into the glories of Viking cesspits and Roman sewers.

The great advantages of urban archaeology are:

1 You will probably be seen on local television.
2 You are never far from home, supplies or medical assistance.
3 You don't have to camp out.
4 There are pubs within easy reach.

The disadvantages are that there are always lots of passers-by gawping at you and asking irritating questions, and even worse, your family and friends can come and embarrass you in front of the other diggers.

The showcase of urban archaeology is the work in York, which has led to the money-spinning reconstruction called the Jorvik Centre (Jorvik being the Viking word for York), where an endless queue of tourists is taken in electric cars or 'time capsules' round a mock-up of a Viking settlement built on the actual site. There are dummies in costume, animatronic figures, sound-effects, holographic Viking ghosts, and even appropriate smells (children especially like the latrine).

If confronted by denigrators of this type of thing, you should applaud its profits and its contribution to bringing the past to life vividly for the general public. If faced with a Jorvik admirer, however, you can wryly observe that it has done for archaeology what Mills & Boon have done for English literature.

EXPERIMENTAL ARCHAEOLOGY

One of the most entertaining branches of archaeology, this involves using ancient implements – or making and using replicas of them – to learn about their functions, capabilities, effectiveness, residues, etc. This gives you a chance to blow Tutankhamun's trumpets, steer an ox-drawn plough, fire arrows, throw spears, attack colleagues with bronze swords, burn down buildings, and still call it scholarly research.

It can have its risky aspects: in the 19th century a certain Dr Robert Ball of Dublin tested some Irish horns of the Late Bronze Age, blew too hard, burst a blood vessel and died. Even today, makers of replica stone tools can be recognised by their chipped spectacles and the bandaids on their fingers.

Bluffers should refer disparagingly to:

a the unreliability, and
b the irrelevance of the results of short-term experiments by unpractised hands.

Archaeology covers such immense periods of time that it tends to be concerned with long-term trends – a century is a brief moment to archaeologists unless they are waiting on the end of a Customer Services helpline. Very few archaeological sites are 'frozen in time', giving an insight into short-term behaviour: Pompeii is one such site, where the end came so suddenly that people have been found doing all kinds of things they never meant posterity to see; and shipwrecks form another kind of 'time capsule'.

You can make the same objections to the equally short-term data acquired in:

ETHNOARCHAEOLOGY

One of the most recent branches of the subject, this is an excellent means of getting an exotic adventure holiday in a remote location. It involves picking on some unsuspecting group of people (hunter-gatherers, simple villagers, sheep farmers, etc.) – preferably in the Third World or Alaska. You then go and live among them for a while, taking note of how and when they make and use things, and how and when they break and discard them.

The victims are expected to tolerate nosy foreigners with notebooks and cameras camping on their doorstep and following them to the shops, workplace, kitchen, dining room and dustbin. Surprisingly, very few ethnoarchaeologists are violently attacked.

After figuring out what you think is going on with the use and discard of objects (you should never stay around long enough to master the language) you return to your desk and use these brief studies to make sweeping generalisations about what people in the past and in totally different environments must have done.

ARCHAEOACOUSTICS

A fairly recent arrival on the scene, and another ideal area for bluffing, this involves testing the acoustic properties of a whole range of sites – decorated caves and rock shelters, burial chambers, Mesoamerican pyramid stairs, and so forth. It is a worthwhile attempt to tackle a hitherto neglected aspect of the past – the sounds made by our forebears, either with their voices or with musical instruments – and one can have great fun clapping, chanting, singing or playing music, while carefully measuring the variations in acoustics in different places. The problem, of course, is that we have absolutely no idea what kinds of sounds were made, or how loudly. Some caves do seem to have decorated panels in places with excellent acoustics; and some burial chambers resonate at the frequencies of the adult male voice. But does this necessarily mean that men (or women with deep voices) chanted here? Or that this was a purposeful factor in a monument's construction? As the bluffer can point out, were bottles designed to hum when you blow across the top?

ARCHAEOASTRONOMY

This approach to the past focuses on actual – or imagined – links between archaeological monuments or imagery and the heavens. Such theories go back to the early years of the subject, being applied to the pyramids, Stonehenge, and many other sites. In some cases the links are pretty solid – for example, the window over the doorway of the megalithic chambered tomb of New Grange in Ireland: at dawn on the winter solstice, the rising sun shines through that window and down the passage. Or at least it does so on the very rare occasions when the sun is visible in an Irish winter. Other claims are far more tenuous – probably every stone circle has been linked to something in the heavens (sun, moon, constellations); but, as sceptics have often remarked, there are so many things up there that almost any monument or circle could be linked to one or more of them by pure chance.

There have been many rather silly claims over the years, involving either an enormous bluff or a lot of wishful thinking. Things reached some kind of extreme in the late 1960s and early 1970s – the apogee of the Space Race – when Stonehenge was seen as an accurate eclipse predictor. But there has always been a tendency to want to see clusters of cupmarks on dolmens as constellations.

One particularly durable myth which the bluffer can have fun with is the obsession in a few quarters of seeing Ice Age cave art as depicting constellations. For some reason it is almost always Lascaux Cave in France's Dordogne which suffers this indignity, probably because its big bull depictions are inevitably thought to represent Taurus. The bluffer can point out that, if Ice Age people were so interested in the heavens, they might conceivably have produced at least one recognisable image of the sun or moon, but they never did.

GENDER ARCHAEOLOGY

Gender Archaeology is aimed at making women visible in the past and escaping archaeology's traditional androcentric biases. Sisters are doing it for themselves, and Men-archaeology is changing into Menarche-ology. But is there a vas deferens between them? Sexism rubs both ways, after all.

'Since archaeology is about all the traces of past human behaviour, it follows that everything thrown away – right up to this morning – can be counted as archaeological material'

INDUSTRIAL ARCHAEOLOGY AND GARBAGE

Since archaeology is about all the traces of past human behaviour, it follows that everything thrown away – right up to this morning – can be counted as archaeological material. Thus a lot of very dedicated people devote their efforts to recording and preserving the relics of the recent industrial past (factories, machinery, mines, bridges, canals, etc.) to make sure that there is something left of it all for future archaeologists to study.

This means that broken fridges, discarded furniture, clapped-out televisions and empty bottles can be argued to be archaeological artifacts. Even the material you consign to your dustbin – your own private little archaeological midden – may still attract the attention of some earnest seekers of data. In Arizona for some years they suffered the aptly named 'Garbage Project', whereby zealous archaeology students poked about in citizens' trash-cans, classifying and quantifying what was thrown away.

This was supposed to give some insights into how

and when people discard things (see Ethnoarchaeology on page 53), but, as any bluffer can point out, with only the faintest of smirks, how empty cans of dogmeat and used light bulbs can tell us much about any period in the past was not readily apparent to folk outside Arizona.

MUSEUM WORK

Finally, many archaeologists are based in museums, where their work entails:

a looking after collections of objects that nobody ever studies
b putting on exhibitions, and
c thinking up ways to amuse and instruct the hordes of screaming schoolchildren inflicted on them by desperate teachers.

Their lives are also blighted by occasional lunatics, and by an endless stream of citizens demanding to have some object identified which they have dug up in the garden or found on the beach. Not unnaturally a great many archaeologists encountered in the field are museum people who have managed a fleeting escape.

DECIPHERMENT

A dying art, as most early scripts have now been deciphered, this is now largely restricted to figuring out what a doctor has written on your prescription, or to secretaries trying to transcribe the scrawl they have been handed. However, in the last couple of centuries it was all the rage, with many kinds of brainteasing puzzles to be cracked around the world.

Jean François Champollion (1790–1832) was one of the best codebreakers. He wrote a book at the age of 12, and by 13 was reading Arabic, Syriac and Coptic, so one can imagine what an insufferable little prodigy he must have been. In 1808 he started work on the Rosetta Stone (which had identical texts in Egyptian scripts and in Greek) and by 1822 had mastered the decipherment of hieroglyphics. Most other decipherers were less fortunate and, instead of having a handy crib of that type, had to start from scratch.

One ancient script that merits the attention of bluffers is that of the Indus civilisation, since it has still not been cracked, so whatever you say about it nobody knows whether you're right or wrong. An even more obscure one is the Rongo Rongo script of Easter Island which only survives as engraved characters on 25 pieces of wood. The modern islanders have occasionally been asked to translate these texts, but tend to come up with something different every time, which means they are pretty good bluffers themselves.

DATING

Scientists are responsible for the invaluable service of providing archaeology with an absolute chronology. Archaeologists give them bits of charcoal, bone, pottery and so forth, and the boffins work their magic and tell the archaeologists how old these objects are. The physicists must feel very popular, as people keep asking them for dates; meeting physics has transformed archaeology's life.

Bluffers only need know the rudiments of a couple of major methods with impressive names:

Dendrochronology
The scientific method of tree dating. Trees grow by annual rings, and since the thickness of each ring varies with the climatic conditions of the year (rich growth in favourable years, etc.) an unbroken series of rings can be built up and extended back for centuries by 'overlapping' identical sequences preserved on modern and ancient timbers. After that, any bit of hardwood found in the area can have its rings checked against the master sequence and its precise age established. This is the archaeological version of calculating by logs.

Thermoluminescence
There is no need to know exactly how this works. Just be aware that it is mainly used to date pottery. It appears that you can figure out how long ago an object was heated up by measuring the amount of light it gives off when reheated. It is not thought to work for left-overs, but you can date food by:

Radiocarbon dating
This method is used on organic substances, and measures the minuscule amount of the radioactive isotope Carbon 14 left in them – after an organism's death, the amount of C14 it contains diminishes steadily, together with the

volume of junk mail it receives. Radiocarbon dates are a paradise for bluffers. They comprise a figure followed by a plus-or-minus sign and another figure: for example, 2450 ± 80 BP means that the age of the object in years may be between 2,530 and 2,370 years before the present – but there is only a 68% chance that it lies within this span.

Few people can remember radiocarbon dates with any accuracy, so you can usually get away with any figure that sounds in the right order of magnitude. If challenged, say yours is a calibrated figure (i.e. corrected because of the various complicated ways in which radiocarbon is inaccurate). There have been many attempts to produce standardised 'calibration curves' (by dating objects and tree rings of known age and seeing how wrong C14 is in each case), and each is different.

When confronted with a radiocarbon date, the bluffer can resort to several ploys:

a Question its accuracy (if uncalibrated), or that of its calibration.
b Enquire what material the date was produced from. Dates from shell, for example, are notoriously inaccurate.
c Point out that a single radiocarbon date is not much use anyway: these days only a whole series of them is considered reliable.

In addition, any date can be called into question simply by casting doubt on the way in which the sample was collected, and suggesting that it may have been contaminated in some way. Very few archaeological dates can stand up to this sort of scrutiny, and your opponent will have to yield to your rigorous scientific standards or risk looking either dangerously dogmatic or sloppy.

In recent years, a new paradise for bluffers has arisen in the form of 'Bayesian statistics' – very few people actually understand what this impressive term means, but suffice it to say that it is a great smoke-and-mirrors method and pretext for retaining the radiocarbon dates that you like, and discarding the ones you don't, while appearing to be strictly objective all the while.

INTERPRETATION

There are two basic trends in archaeology of which the bluffer should be aware.

1 The dates for various inventions (such as pottery) or events (e.g. the arrival of humans in Australia) are constantly being pushed back.
2 The places of origin of different archaeological features, including people themselves, shift around the globe as new discoveries are made. As Breuil (see page 107) said of human origins, 'The cradle of humanity is on casters.'

So the art of interpreting archaeological evidence is to leave yourself room for manoeuvre in the light of future discovery.

The shortcomings of archaeological interpretation should be readily apparent: indeed, it has been described as 'the recovery of unobservable behaviour patterns from indirect traces in bad samples'. The astute bluffer can drive home the point with a parable about some archaeologist far in the future trying to make sense of an early 21st-century site – buildings marked with golden arches would be identified as places of worship where ritual meals were prepared; the main deities are clearly a mouse in red pants and white gloves, and a group of yellow humans (their images are found everywhere, especially on clothing); and the Coca-Cola bottle would be a phallic symbol or a female figurine according to the interpreter's predilections.

ANCIENT DNA

Another bunch of boffins are currently studying ancient genetic material – it's a new toy which has become available, and hardly a week goes by without some new announcement about the populating of the New World (these claims usually contradict each other), or the domestication of dogs, or the fate of the Neanderthals. As occurred with radiocarbon dating which was such an unexpected and incredible addition to the archaeological arsenal after the war, it is highly probable that many mistakes are being made in this initial rush of excitement, and that many of the claims will need to be corrected or discarded in due course. But the accomplished bluffer will argue that this is indeed a revolution in archaeology, and that things are going to change rapidly and drastically from now on in our accounts of the past. One example to mention is that for decades scholars referred to 'the Beaker Folk', a people who came into Britain and who brought metalworking, a new pottery vessel and a new style of burial with them. Then in the 1970s such claims began to be dismissed as simplistic, and all talk switched to movement and dissemination not of people but only of ideas and fashions and, perhaps, of a kind of beverage which was drunk from the Beaker vessels, rather like the spread of Coca-Cola. Now, however, thanks to DNA analysis of lots of skeletons, the Beaker Folk are back and this time they mean business – it seems they did exist after all, they did come into Britain from mainland Europe, and what's more they seem to have totally displaced or replaced the earlier population of prehistoric British.

At the same time, many people – especially in America – are excitedly paying money to companies which offer them a read-out of their genetic material, so they can find out what percentage of Neanderthal they have in them, or where in the world their ancestors may have originated. The more cynical bluffer might point out that these paying customers have no way of knowing how accurate or valid the results supplied might be; the only way to check would be to spend yet more dollars and send their DNA to a different company and compare the results. There is money in your genes.

Ⓑ

'It is advisable, even if you have a pronounced sense of the absurd, to appear to take the past very seriously. After all, it's the only one we've got.'

THE OUTER LIMITS

CURSES

It is popularly believed, thanks to movies, comic strips and tabloids, that archaeologists who disturb tombs or sacred sites fall prey to dire curses. The most famous case is that of the tomb of Tutankhamun, since Lord Carnarvon (who financed the work) died a few months after the tomb was discovered in 1922. Bluffers should scoff at this belief, suggesting that Tutankhamun might have devised a more spectacular death for Carnarvon than falling victim to pneumonia (in fact it is likely that his death was due to inhalation, in a passage leading to the tomb, of a fungus in the dried dust from bat droppings).

You can also point out that Howard Carter, who actually found and stripped the tomb and disturbed the body, died a natural death some 17 years later.

Many deaths following archaeological disturbance of tombs and other sites can in fact be attributed to a more mundane cause: archaeology is a dirty business, sifting through old rubbish and decayed organic matter.

It would be surprising if there were not occasional germs and spores lurking somewhere in the debris, and since archaeologists are not known for cleanliness they may well eat their on-site snacks with hands that are less than spotless. Excavators therefore recommend tetanus shots and carbolic soap.

A variety of other curses can afflict archaeologists, especially in the field:

a colds, chills or worse (especially in Britain)
b blisters, sunstroke, collapsing trenches
c the runs (known as Montezuma's revenge)
d angry locals
e site-looters
f lack of finds (the 'barren site' curse) and, worst of all,
g running out of alcohol.

A different kind of modern curse is the rise of an enthusiastic army of amateurs with metal-detectors. For some reason these people get their excitement from digging up old scraps of metal or coins, and an even bigger and more understandable thrill out of finding valuable hoards of treasure. If faced with such people, the archaeological bluffer should preach patronisingly against their ever touching known archaeological sites, and urge them to restrict their activities to shorelines and spoilheaps (though most archaeologists would, in fact, prefer them to work in minefields).

If confronting a professional archaeologist, however, the bluffer will speak up on behalf of the responsible and careful metal-detector enthusiast, while taking pains to condemn the majority. Archaeologists can get quite overwrought about this question of digging up metal, and wish people would leave it to rust in peace until it can be excavated properly in its full archaeological context.

Many feel that anyone who selfishly plunders a piece of the past (whether a site-looter or an archaeologist who fails to publish a report) has stolen something irreplaceable from all humanity. It is advisable therefore, even if you have a pronounced sense of the absurd, to appear to take the past very seriously. After all, it's the only one we've got.

FAKES

People are extremely easy to fool, and archaeologists are no exception. Over the years, great numbers of them have fallen prey to unscrupulous individuals and have believed in the authenticity of fakes.

In 1991, a young history student in the Basque region of northern Spain claimed to have found Ice Age paintings in a cave called Zubialde. Their freshness, clumsiness and sheer ugliness caused most specialists to suspect fakery (one might say it was a site for eyesores). This was confirmed when the paint was found to contain a fragment of a well-known brand of green plastic kitchen sponge.

Astonishingly, the Spanish Basque region was also the scene of a tragic-comic episode a few years ago during excavations of a well-known Roman city called Veleia. A sealed 3rd-century AD layer began producing quantities of potsherds, and many of these proved to have inscriptions engraved on them. Some had Basque words on them – but whereas the earliest known medieval texts in Basque can only be understood by linguistic specialists, these could be understood by any Basque in the street today; others had Egyptian hieroglyphics on them, including the names of Nefertiti and Nefertari, in forms only adopted by Egyptologists in the 19th century; and some Christian motifs were also found, including a crucifixion scene in which the notice on the cross, instead of 'INRI', said 'RIP'. The potsherds were genuine, but clearly the inscriptions were the work of mischievous hands back at the lab. Any site may produce one bizarre piece of evidence; it may even produce two totally different kinds of bizarre evidence; but three different kinds from the same layer should ring alarm bells. In Japan in the 1980s and 1990s an amateur archaeologist, Shinichi Fujimura, was renowned for his 'divine hands' because he had discovered a whole series of stone tools dating back to 700,000 years ago. But in 2000 a newspaper published photos of him digging holes to bury tools, and it emerged that he was a complete fraud. An investigation concluded that all of the 168 sites he was known to have dug had been faked, which meant that much of what was known about the Japanese Palaeolithic had to be rewritten. Even worse, it is believed that he also planted fake artifacts at other sites as yet unexcavated, meaning that there are 'archaeological time bombs' awaiting future Japanese archaeologists. Fujimura was hospitalised for mental illness, but then came out and changed his name. Sadly, another Japanese archaeologist who was wrongly accused of fakery around the same time committed suicide because of the dishonour.

You should know that one of the earliest known fakers was an Englishman, Edward Simpson (1815–*c*.1875), ultimately known as **Flint Jack** and also, less felicitously, as Fossil Willie. He became a prolific forger of flint tools, ancient implements and pottery, often passing them off to experts and amateurs alike as genuine specimens. More of a practical joker than a crook, he just liked taking people for a ride, and eventually took to giving public displays of his expertise. Flint Jack was something of an 'archaeologist manqué', as he was extremely scruffy, had a terrible weakness for drink, and died in poverty.

One of the earliest known fakers was an Englishman, Edward Simpson, ultimately known as 'Flint Jack' and also, less felicitously, as 'Fossil Willie'.

Controversy raged for decades in France over a site called Glozel, dug in the 1920s, which contained a set of amazing and obvious fakes, supposedly showing that Ice Age carvings, Bronze Age pots and Near Eastern inscribed clay tablets all co-existed in this one spot near Vichy. Yet a few archaeologists are still reluctant to dismiss the site, and many non-archaeologists still uphold it as an example of blinkered archaeology not wanting to face up to awkward facts and an unknown civilisation. One American even 'deciphered' the Glozel tablets, and claimed they showed the place was a bazaar selling ointments, amulets, and devices to ensure sexual potency.

The most famous fakery occurred in England in 1912 when **Piltdown Man**, a 'missing link', was trumpeted as the earliest Englishman. It says much for the archaeologists' lack of humour that they still did not smell a rat when Piltdown produced a bone implement shaped like a cricket bat.

PSEUDO-ARCHAEOLOGY

Archaeologists have long been accustomed to dealing with harmless individuals obsessed by the fate of the Ten Lost Tribes of Israel, the location of the lost continent of Mu, or the bizarre idea that everything in the British landscape can be joined together along straight lines or in the form of signs of the zodiac. Most museums and other such institutions are pestered by their share of cranks who believe that Atlantis was in Glasgow or that the number of blocks in the Great Pyramid is mysteriously equal to the number of words in the Bible. One man, however, took this kind of thing to new heights (or depths, depending on your viewpoint), and in a book like this deserves a section of his own as the epitome of archaeological bluffing.

An obscure Swiss hotel manager, twice convicted of fraud and embezzlement, **Erich von Däniken** in 1968 wrote a book called *Chariots of the Gods* which, together with its very similar successors, sold over 25 million copies in 32 countries – probably more than all archaeology books combined.

His ideas were not original, but have become associated with his name. Put simply, they ascribe anything in the human past that looks difficult or bizarre (big monuments, enigmatic drawings) to visitors from outer space. Regardless of whether he believed this 'ancient astronaut' concept, he made it far better known and more widely accepted than any archaeological theory, the ultimate achievement for a bluffer. He even had his own successful and lucrative theme park in Switzerland for a while. Few scholars bothered to write books to counter the theory, partly because they felt it beneath their dignity and partly because such books never sell. As it would be unethical to let these falsehoods go unchallenged, you should have a few basic facts at hand – but only a few, as the typical von Däniken fan is the kind of person whose lips move while reading. You will not need to study his books in depth: a mere skim through one of them, or just the picture captions, will suffice to show you his approach and his uses of sleight-of-hand.

If, on the other hand, faced with someone who is already anti-von Däniken, you are forced to find something positive to say about him, stress that his books are useful aids for teaching students how not to write, and how to recognise:

a   false logic
b   tricks of presentation
c   blatant distortions of the truth, and
d   sly selection of facts.

Then swiftly admit, before being challenged, that many archaeological texts can serve the same purpose.

WEB LOONIES

The rise of the internet has had incalculable effects on archaeology, as on every other aspect of modern life. Enormous quantities of useful information can now be found with a mere click of a mouse or a swipe of a finger, and the days are long gone when a few powerful institutions such as elite universities, encyclopedias and leading news organisations were the gatekeepers of scientific information. The internet has democratised access to data. However, one should always be aware of the fact that among the millions of pages of information there are not merely oceans of bluffing, but also a huge abundance of delusional rubbish, wishful thinking, and cretinous fantasy, and it is not always easy for the ill-informed, the gullible or the unwary to figure out which is which. Wikipedia, which has already become THE 'go-to' source of information for many people, not least students, is well known for its occasional errors and even practical jokes.

In the not-too-distant past, one could recognise letters arriving from loonies, as they were almost always written in green ink, for some reason. Now, however, they have gone digital – online anonymity is apparently irresistible – and email is their communication device of choice, and so one can only assess the degree of eccentricity or even insanity after reading a paragraph or two (or, in some cases, just a few words). On the one hand, such missives provide a never-ending source of bemusement and entertaining anecdotes; on the other, it is startling and worrying to discover the abysmally low level of intelligence, common sense and general knowledge of a large portion of the world-wide-web community. This is one of the many reasons why the internet is so precious to the accomplished bluffer.

If you want to find common-sense archaeology on the web, then sites such as badarchaeology.com are a godsend to those who are capable of separating the valid from the ridiculous – it is run by people who describe themselves as 'angry archaeologists', a truly fearsome concept. There are also lots of discussion groups online, devoted to every archaeological subject under the sun. But if you just want a good laugh, then you can have endless fun surfing the net, and finding anything and everything – lost super-civilisations, giant human skeletons excavated in Saudi Arabia, and even a video by someone in Japan who believes that Easter Island is entirely man-made. For those who flee screaming from social media, it is impossible to assess adequately the importance of these phenomena in modern archaeology – presumably the younger generation finds them a source of great entertainment and interest, and a valuable asset. Any bluffer who is likewise an outsider from these media can claim to agree with the widely-held view that Twitter is a medium of communication designed for the vapid, the deranged and the self-obsessed....

———————— *ß* ————————

*'Stealing from one author is plagiarism,
but from many is research . .'*

ARCHAEOLOGY IN PRINT

Although there are now innumerable books and journals devoted to archaeology, only a small percentage are owed to a desire to disseminate knowledge to colleagues, let alone to the public that usually footed the bill for the work. The vast majority of archaeological publications are produced with one aim in mind: self-advancement.

When applying for jobs or research funds, an archaeologist has to supply a list of publications with the curriculum vitae, and an impressive list can make a big difference to promotion prospects: never mind the quality, feel the length. Size does matter in academic circles.

Since few archaeologists manage to keep up a stream of innovative and varied studies, most employ a great deal of bluff in this area. It may entail publishing reams of meaningless abstraction with no possible application or relevance to the real world (see Theoretical Archaeology); or, more commonly, endlessly recycling the same piece of work: this is known as the 'Enid Blyton Syndrome', and enables one to achieve a massive list of publications with minimum effort. As long as the titles and journals are different, you are home and dry – referees cannot read everything, and most papers are read by only a few people.

So, most of the time, this bluff is easy to carry off. Indeed, it is self-perpetuating, because the more you publish the easier it becomes to get published; and anyone outside the system or with something new and original to say will often be refereed by the Blytonians and thus weeded out. It also means that, at conferences, everyone already knows what everyone else is going to say, so can spend more time propping up the bar.

Papers usually have to be given at conferences in order to get grants to attend. You also need to bluff the funding agency into believing that the conference is of enormous importance to your subject. In fact, however, little new is ever said at such events, and their main functions are for socialising, gossiping, philandering, job hunting, and generally proving that you are still around.

Books are a more complex problem than papers, as they usually take some time to research and write. Once again, however, there are some notable short-cuts for the expert bluffer:

1 Learn to witter at great length (see Theoretical Archaeology on page 22).
2 Synthesise the work of others (stealing from one author is plagiarism, but from many is research). Or better still,
3 Synthesise your own work by lumping together some of your old articles between hard covers.

The lucky few who bluff their way to fame will even find that publishers are keen to pay money to put their names on the covers of books to which they have contributed only a token preface.

Another crafty way to get your name on the front of a book is to edit it: this simply entails writing to a number of people and asking if they would like to contribute a chapter or a paper to a prestigious new volume. Most are so flattered to be asked, and so desperate to add another item to their publications list, that they rush to comply, and, hey presto, a book of other people's hard work comes out under your name. One or two archaeologists on both sides of the Atlantic are so practised at this dodge that they bring out at least one edited book per year. They may be packed with hot air, but quality of content is irrelevant to the perception of productivity.

Yet another cunning way of advancing your career is to write up somebody else's famous excavation, left unpublished after their death, and hence take all the credit for their work. This means you don't need to do any of that tedious digging and recording yourself, and if the work proves to contain serious errors, you can escape criticism by putting all the blame on the excavator and his/her team. A further bonus is that, once you have published your version of what was found, it is highly unlikely that anyone will bother to go back to the original archive to check. And as you are the principal author, all subsequent work will have to cite you as the authority on the project.

PUBLISHING RUSES

Hedging

One basic rule in archaeological publishing is to avoid dogmatism, and to fill your work with the words 'maybe', 'perhaps', and 'possibly'. This enables you to make an orderly and dignified retreat in case of attack or being proved wrong.

Obfuscating

Another way to sidestep criticism is to make your prose so obscure and tortuous that nobody, including yourself, is quite sure at the end of it what you have been saying. Using neatly circular arguments and runic impenetrability, one can achieve maximum semantic chaos with minimum effort. This smokescreen effect, particularly common in theoretical work, is very useful when it turns out that you were wrong, or new finds alter the situation: you can simply claim that you were misunderstood and that you said nothing of the kind.

Padding

Another ruse in print is to include lots of lists and tables which nobody will ever bother to check or read in their entirety, but which serve to make your work seem scholarly and thorough. Similarly, some authors, many of them French, put a long bibliography at the end containing numerous impressive sources – most of which are never actually referred to in the text. It's just window-dressing, but very effective since it is unlikely that anyone will read the whole work and notice the absences.

Non-publication
Some archaeologists get away for years, even decades, without publishing anything of note. This is more serious if they are thereby withholding, from colleagues and the world at large, information which they have dug up or otherwise obtained. Many are the cases around the world, involving some very famous sites, but instead of ostracising the individuals concerned, archaeologists generally treat them with the utmost courtesy and only mutter about them behind their backs.

There are a number of basic reasons for non-publication:

1 **Laziness, lethargy** or **complacency** (primarily among those with tenured jobs who therefore don't have to worry about having their output assessed).
2 **Incompetence.** This takes many forms: some can hardly string two sentences together, let alone produce an accurate report on a piece of work. Others are congenitally untidy, so notes and even finds get lost in the stratigraphy that builds up in their offices and laboratories. One or two have even been known to be so absent-minded that they leave manuscripts, notes and irreplaceable finds on trains or in taxis. There are even cases of important plans and major parts of site archives being left behind in hurriedly-cleared offices or site-huts and caravans, used at the time of the digs, only to be rediscovered decades later.

3 **Terror** – or 'reasons to be fearful'. Some are so thin-skinned that the very thought of laying themselves open to criticism is torture. Of course, the fact that they don't publish is also attacked, but this is considered the lesser of the two evils in a subject where you are guaranteed to be torn to shreds by someone whatever you do.

4 **Being too busy.** New lecturers tend to be given the heaviest teaching load, as well as all the jobs nobody else can stand, such as serving on library committees, marking exam papers and conducting outings to museums. Others are simply too preoccupied with building their careers to pay any attention to little matters like ethics.

5 **The conveyor belt.** Many archaeologists, amazingly, are permitted to keep digging or researching without publishing anything on what they have already done. This soon builds up a huge backlog of data and finds, most of which will never be analysed and processed, let alone published. As a phenomenon it gives an illusion of constant activity. In reality it is the best ruse of all. These days this applies particularly to contract archaeology, where the desire to keep a successful digging team together often leads to an unending stream of excavations, with no time allocated to writing up the results.

Very few archaeologists have ever been known to admit their mistakes, in print at any rate. Even in published retractions, they generally state that their original position was correct, but that circumstances have changed. Thus criticism of their earlier work can be deflected by the comment 'That's what I thought at the time, but I've moved on since then.' You can never actually pin them down to explaining clearly how they view the problem at present. Backtracking, U-turns and shifting goalposts are all too easy to those practised at this kind of manoeuvre. A scientist's duty is to be prepared – even before they are formulated – to one day, without regret, sacrifice his conclusions. But very few do!

Bluffers must always give the impression of being very well read in the subject, not only in their writings but also in conversation. If asked whether you have read some new book, you can plead poverty and claim to be waiting for the paperback (few serious archaeology books ever come out in paperback), and thus steer talk into the ever-worsening problem of grossly overpriced texts. Another effective ploy if asked about a specific book or article is to express enthusiasm, and say that you are terribly busy but dying to read it as soon as your limited spare time permits: then turn the tables by asking your companion's opinion.

SHADES OF GREY

The explosion in recent years in commercial archaeology (particularly in Britain), whereby excavation precedes construction projects, has produced a veritable flood of new information, which in turn has been recorded in a mass of unpublished reports. Whereas, in the past, academic archaeologists excavated and then published their results in journals and monographs, readily available in libraries, nowadays the vast majority of excavations are carried out, and written up, for clients and local government planners, and the resulting reports are then held in private offices or local government buildings – and often not publicly available. As they are not usually for sale or housed in libraries, they are not available on inter-library loan, and are difficult to find and access, so researchers need to travel all over the place to try and consult them. In some cases, archaeological information has become a commodity, and developers control access to it. Fortunately, an ever-increasing proportion is now being placed on the web – in Britain, this entails going to seek refreshment at ADS or the OASIS, with its online library of unpublished fieldwork reports.

These reports are dubbed grey literature – a very apt term because they tend to be produced in an all-purpose style that is tedious to read. In fact it can be heroically tedious, valiantly uninteresting and panoramically bereft of anything to grab one's attention. Indeed it has been said that 'some bits...are barely worth the paper they are printed on'. It occasionally rises to the uninspired. One might even say that it has hidden shallows. It attains a pinnacle of banality that can only be called heroic, and therefore a little bit of it can go a long way – as Mark Twain said, 'I have witnessed and enjoyed the first act of everything which Wagner created. One was quite sufficient.' What is even worse is that these reports are not subject to peer review, their results (such as dating) are often highly provisional, and very few of the finds have been subject to any detailed study or analysis.

SECTS

Sects and cults can block research for decades, having led it down a false trail into a dead end; and yet they do arise in archaeology from time to time, as in any discipline. What generally happens is that someone puts forward a theory, but in such a way as to claim that it is an unquestionable truth, a key to understanding some enigmatic aspect of the past – for example, the meaning of some rock art. All fads attract zealots, who are adept at leaping onto passing bandwagons. Sects have a strong appeal for people who are simultaneously

---

'There is nothing so unthinkable as thought, unless it be the entire absence of thought. . .'

---

self-obsessed and deficient in real personality, while the guru they choose to believe and to follow slavishly is usually a combination of bumbling incompetence and inflated self-importance. Their pet theory is repeatedly and unwaveringly trotted out like a mantra, often amid a grotesque river of drivel that is fascinating for many reasons, none of them pleasant. The gurus never seem to age their act. Indeed, it is hard to understand that years of study can lead to such blinkered ignorance; but it is sadly true that often the people who say the most know the least. There is nothing so unthinkable as thought, unless it be the entire absence of thought;

and everything about such sects is wrong – not just a bit wrong, or bravely wrong, or nearly right, but screamingly, abysmally wrong.

A guru can usually extend his field of operations to the full distance that gullibility will allow. In this respect it is worth remembering that a hugely intelligent man like Arthur Conan Doyle, the creator of Sherlock Holmes's deductive and logical mind, firmly believed that illusionist Harry Houdini had supernormal powers. Even when Houdini assured him that they were all tricks, he persisted in his unshakeable belief – just as followers of an archaeological sect often refuse to abandon them even when its claims are shown to be claptrap. Indeed, they seem to think that abandoning a cause is a worse crime than not sharing the cause at all – rather like in extreme Islam, where an apostate is worse than an infidel. And attacks are often launched against non-believers of a cherished archaeological theory, while its supporters refuse to accept that it is a passing fad rather than a revealed truth. Fortunately, doctrines and dogmas come and go, but the basic data remain.

In some ways, the disciples of a guru could be described as having been brainwashed. But as with jihadists, the term 'brainwashing' should really be reserved for cases where there are brains to be washed – usually, nothing more elaborate has happened than the filling of a vacuum, and if that hadn't been filled by one brand of nonsense, it would have been filled by another. When faced with a disciple of such an archaeological cult, the bluffer can really go to town with a few home truths. For example, all you can be sure of is that anyone who sounds as if he has all the answers hasn't. The golden rule is that there are no golden rules, and all generalisations are dangerous, even this one. Sects and cults are very adept at selecting the facts they like and ignoring those that don't fit their pet theory, while making some truly outrageous claims. But facts do not cease to exist because they are ignored; and extraordinary claims require extraordinary evidence. It is important to keep an open mind, but not so open that your brains fall out. As Karl Popper said, if we are uncritical, we shall always find what we want; we shall look for and find confirmation, and we shall look away from, and not see, whatever might be dangerous to our pet theories.

True science entails ceaseless questioning, scepticism, wanting to know what the evidence is and understanding what the evidence means. And true scholars realise that the more you know, the less you think you know. The most important lesson to be learned from the phenomenon of archaeological sects is: Think for yourself! Assess the evidence for yourself, and don't trust what you hear in lectures or read in texts. (But bluffers should always pretend that they have come to this conclusion themselves, and not picked it up from books like this one.)

CONTRARIANS

The distinguishing mark of people who think for themselves, and of sceptics – and of the British in general – is irreverence towards received ideas. In recent years, however, a new breed of archaeologists has taken this to unnecessary extremes by becoming 'contrarians' – having found that taking the contrary view pays dividends, they seem to make this the tone of their customary discourse. The contrarians make names for themselves simply by inverting established truth (e.g. by claiming, despite massive evidence, that Neanderthals did not bury their dead) – in a cynical ploy to make themselves known. They usually present a stream of random, self-justifying nuggets, plucked from the furthest shores and cul-de-sacs of archaeology, which are then strung together to make some sort of a point. In most cases this is not a lesson or even a coherent opinion. They have little information, only attitudes. It's a contrarian rant, said for effect – or simply a commercial for a book.

Faced with a contrarian, the accomplished bluffer will note that we are all refreshed and challenged by a unique view, and that everyone is entitled to their own opinion – but nobody is entitled to their own fact! Some people seem to be addicted to walking up the down escalator, and denying what seems to be unquestionably established in the eyes of the vast majority of scholars. As Kenneth Galbraith said of economists, the experience of being disastrously wrong is so salutary that no archaeologist should be denied it, and not many are.

PRETENTIOUS, MOI??

Finally, the bluffer can enjoy poking fun at the pretentious members of the archaeological community. In general, pomposity is inversely proportionate to competence, and is a hallmark of small-minded mediocrity. Moderate intelligence is frequently prey to a kind of snobbery which genuine intellectual superiority is careful to avoid. One can encounter endless examples in the writings and pronouncements of the pretentious. One particular favourite is the email in which the writer used the words 'this violates my sense of epistemology' – a wonderful phrase which the bluffer should adopt and introduce into any conversation, as it is guaranteed to floor an opponent.

A different kind of pretentiousness is the use of exotic terms in the mistaken belief that they are correct. One notable and amusing example is the word 'sumptuary', which some American archaeologists employ – as in 'he was accompanied by sumptuary grave goods' – apparently under the impression that it is a cross between 'luxury' and 'sumptuous'. Unfortunately, however, it actually means 'designed to prevent extravagance and luxury'.

Ⱬ

'Anything in archaeology with no obvious function is classed as "ritual".'

SOME NAMES TO KNOW

If, at a party, you are asked what you do, and you confess that you are working on a typology of clay pipes dug up around Stoke Poges, you are not going to enthral your audience for more than 2.5 seconds. All aspiring archaeological bluffers therefore need to know something about the more exotic people and places that do interest others, preferably those which remain enigmatic or controversial and to which there is no complete answer. Here are a few to choose from:

STONEHENGE

One of the very few British archaeological sites that the whole world has heard of, this unique structure on Salisbury Plain comprises a 'henge' (a circular area bounded by earth banks and a ditch) with huge megaliths set upright inside it. The biggest stones even have horizontal slabs set on top of them (two uprights and a lintel form a 'trilithon'), using a mortise and tenon system – i.e. bumps on the uprights fit into corresponding hollows in the lintels. It is not known exactly how the horizontal stones could be fitted there, though visiting astronauts are unlikely to have been recruited.

The biggest stones (sarsens) are local, but the bluestones (actually bluish with pink flecks) are thought to have been brought from Wales – perhaps there was a discount there for bulk purchase. Excavators have divided the site's development, spanning a period from about 3000 to 1600 BC, into a whole series of phases (I, II, IIIa,b,c) which nobody can remember (IIIb or not IIIb? That is the question). If asked about these, you can neatly sidestep the issue by claiming to disagree with the sequence and explaining that you have not yet had time to read the excavation reports in order to assess the evidence for yourself.

Stonehenge is generally thought to be a ritual site (anything in archaeology with no obvious function is classed as ritual). At the moment, rival theories are slugging it out in the literature – one contends that this was a place for the dead, while another claims that, on the contrary, it was a place of healing, rather like a prehistoric Lourdes, perhaps. Of course, there may be some truth in all these views, as well as many others that have not yet occurred to anyone! Basically, the site and its surroundings have been researched to death, to the point of boredom of all except those involved in the studies, who can still attract media attention and hefty funding.

The monument clearly has some astronomical significance as it is aligned on the midsummer sunrise. However, it pre-dates the Druids by many centuries, and there is no evidence for a link either with their religion or with human sacrifice. This does not stop a bunch of people in white nighties turning up there every June to perform some pseudo-Druidic ceremonies.

In recent years Stonehenge has also become the focus of a midsummer invasion by hippies and travellers, who presumably venerate it as the earliest rock group, and who gather there to give thanks for the rising sun and their Social Security cheques.

'SEAHENGE'

Found in 1998, this Bronze Age monument in Norfolk comprised 55 split oak trees forming a circle around a massive upturned oak stump with its roots pointing upwards. Inevitably it was assumed to be ritual. The monument was originally located in marshland near the coast, but rising sea levels eventually drowned it. If nothing else, it shows that prehistoric people close to the seaside always had their trunks at the ready.

CARNAC

A collection of thousands of prehistoric standing stones in Brittany, and not to be confused with Karnak (a huge temple in Egypt), they run in rows for miles across the landscape, looking like the endless vistas of termite mounds in northern Australia. Bluffers should, however, use such similes carefully, or impressionable listeners will automatically assume that the Carnac megaliths were erected by a party of homesick Aborigines.

Sites like Carnac are bread and butter to the bluffer since nobody has the faintest idea what they were. One early theory was that there is treasure buried under one stone, and all the others serve as decoys. Another speculated that each stone served as a wind-break for a tent in a Roman camp. The monument is, as usual, assumed to have been ritual, and inevitably thought to have some astronomical function, but basically your guess is as good as anyone else's. You should know that these standing stones are called menhirs. If this brings up the Asterix books, point out that, while funny, the books are archaeologically bogus because they bring prehistoric megaliths thousands of years forward to Roman times. This may brand you a spoilsport, but will confirm your credentials as a stickler for factual accuracy.

THE TERRACOTTA ARMY

The biggest find of the 1970s, it was, as usual, made not by archaeologists but by Chinese peasants drilling for water. What they found near Xian (pronounced She-an) turned out to be thousands of life-size clay figures of soldiers and horses arranged in ranks. They were made to guard, in death, the Emperor Qin Shihuangdi (3rd century BC), who is buried under a huge mound some distance away. This strange practice was, at least, an improvement on slaughtering people to do the job in the afterlife: in any case, who could you get to massacre your whole army?

The troops were clearly well equipped and armed, demonstrating that the Chinese army had not yet gone to pot by this time. Anxious archaeologists are wondering if they can also expect a terracotta navy to turn up.

NAZCA

An intriguing mystery, this desert in Peru is covered by thousands of straight lines that go for miles, running parallel or criss-crossing, and by scores of huge outline drawings of animals, birds, fish, spiders, etc. They were made centuries ago by moving stones aside to reveal the lighter earth beneath, and only make sense from the air. Maria Reiche, a German mathematician, spent decades trying to prove that they have an astronomical function; it goes without saying that they are generally considered ritual. Von Däniken insists the site is a kind of airport for flying saucers (but why on earth should spaceships require runways?). Others propose the Nazcans had the knowledge and technology to go up in balloons (like many archaeologists, they knew a lot about hot air). Bluffers might try suggesting that the Nazca people were just extremely tall. There is no evidence for this, but there isn't any for astronauts or balloons either.

AZTECS AND INCAS

Many people, including most beginning students, find it hard to remember which of these two peoples lived in Peru and which in Mexico, and whether they were destroyed by Cortes or by Pizarro. Bluffers can keep these basic facts at their fingertips by recalling that:

- Inca and Peru both have four letters, Peru and Pizarro both begin with a P.
- Aztecs, Mexico and Cortes all have six letters.

The devastation of these two great civilisations by the Spanish lust for gold is one of the most tragic episodes in human history. Some believe that the devastation of much of Spain by uncouth holiday makers' lust for sun, sea and sangria is a delayed divine retribution.

The Incas made impressive temples and forts of enormous blocks beautifully fitted together (though probably not by passing astronauts). They had heaps of gold, but no writing: they used knotted string instead, and even Champollion would have had his work cut out to decipher those. Their most famous site is Machu Picchu (pronounced Matchoo Pitchoo), which sounds like someone sneezing.

The Aztecs are associated with big temple platforms like pyramids, and with sacrificing thousands of enemies in order to feed the ravenous appetite of their gods. If pressed on the topic, you can deflect questions by mentioning other groups in Mesoamerica (not Mexico, please) such as the Toltecs, Mixtecs, Zapotecs, Chichimecs and Maya. Only a New World specialist would know how all these fit together spatially and chronologically, and, as such specialists are very thin on the ground outside America, you are pretty safe to speculate at will. The most famous Mesoamerican site to drop into conversation is Chichén Itzá, which also sounds like a sneeze. If you find you get Machu Picchu and Chichén Itzá mixed up, figure out your own way to remember which is which – we can't hand you everything on a plate.

EASTER ISLAND (RAPA NUI)

Most people are familiar with the gigantic stone heads dotted around this tiny speck of land in the Pacific, though bluffers will dismiss talk of 'heads' and call them 'statues' since the figures actually include the torso, but many have become buried up to the neck over the years. It is amazing that, when a report on a recent excavation of two statues buried to the chin was posted on the web, it led to a frenzy of internet activity, with millions of people around the world expressing astonishment at the 'revelation' that the 'Easter Island heads' had bodies! Had these idiots never seen any photos of the full statues standing on platforms?

Unfortunately, most people are also familiar with von Däniken's claims that the volcanic rock here is too hard to be carved by stone tools, and that in any case there were no trees to provide rollers and levers to move these monsters. Consequently it must have been (surprise, surprise) astronauts again.

In fact, the rock is exceptionally soft and easy to carve, there are thousands of hammer-stones and hundreds of unfinished statues still in the quarry, and there is ample evidence from pollen and other botanical remains that the whole island was originally covered in big palm trees, admirably suitable for use as rollers, etc.

The inhabitants thought their island was the whole world (the rest having disappeared in a flood), so it was rash of them to devastate the place, first by massacring and driving away its rich array of birds, and then by cutting down all the trees. Whoever cut down the very last tree on the island knew it was the last, but still cut it down anyway, presumably not to cries of 'For he's a jolly good feller'.

Bluffers should try to steer conversations about Easter Island* away from the statues to the amazing rock-carvings of vulvas. In Rapa Nui culture, the clitoris was deliberately lengthened from an early age, and girls were expected to straddle two rocks to display them to priests at certain ceremonies. The longest were honoured by being immortalised in stone, and their proud owners would get the best warriors as husbands. Modern women might share a similar ambition, but would probably feel that going to those lengths to achieve it is stretching the point.

*Always use the islanders' own names for it, Rapa Nui and 'Te Pito o Te Henua' which means 'Navel of the World').

AUSTRALIA

Australian archaeology as a whole is a valuable area for the bluffer as it's only been underway for a few decades, and hardly anyone outside Australia knows anything about it. Dazzle your audience by mentioning such sites as Lake Mungo, Kutikina, Kow Swamp and Beginners' Luck Cave. It is also one of the richest areas for rock art, with thousands of sites and millions of motifs. Some sites are still sacred to the Aborigines who give them evocative names such as Darangingnarri ('Walk over to woman with open legs'). The accomplished bluffer can mention one of the great enigmas of prehistory – i.e. the fact that circa 3,000 years ago, when Tasmania was separated from the mainland, its inhabitants subsequently appear to have stopped eating fish.

CHAUVET CAVE

One of the most blatant examples of archaeological bluffing in recent years is this most beautiful decorated cave in south-east France. When first discovered in 1994 by three speleologists (see page 123) its art was assigned to various phases of the last Ice Age on the basis of very sound arguments of style, content, technique, and so forth. But charcoal taken from a couple of the drawings produced incredibly early radiocarbon results, supposedly making this the 'oldest art in the world'. Alas, it has become very clear that the dating was defective and that the original estimates were correct. But to admit this would put so much egg on so many faces that the truth is still being stifled by the authorities, and the erroneous claims have now entered all textbooks and popular works. Never let the facts get in the way of a good bluff! Another astonishing facet of the saga is that, for petty and vindictive reasons, the authorities, after 20 years, tried to rename the cave. It was named after Jean-Marie Chauvet, leader of the three discoverers, and everyone has known it as the 'Grotte Chauvet' ever since. But the authorities wanted to give it the much catchier title of the 'Grotte de Vallon Pont d'Arc, Ardèche'. The accomplished bluffer will remark that this is rather like trying to rename Stonehenge as the 'Wiltshire stone circle', and just as pointless and fatuous.

THE ICEMAN

Found in 1991, high in the Italian Alps, the Iceman is the oldest intact body discovered thus far, dating to about 5,300 years ago. Nicknamed Ötzi, he rapidly triggered some amazing stories – one woman reportedly claimed it was her father who had disappeared in the mountains; apparently she recognised him from the press photographs (it must be assumed that he hadn't aged well). Once his antiquity had been established, a number of women allegedly volunteered to be impregnated with any frozen sperm that might be found in his body. Even more bizarrely, a gay magazine in Austria claimed that sperm had been discovered in his anal canal, but that scientists were too embarrassed to publish this 'fact'. Needless to say, it was rubbish, and he had no such 'frozen assets'.

The Austrian archaeologist who became responsible for the first study of the Iceman was called Konrad Spindler – he got the job not through any expertise but simply because he happened to be around at the time of the discovery. One of his first tasks was to make an inventory of the clothing and equipment found with the body – this was inevitably dubbed Spindler's List.

The bluffer can point out the sobering fact that – despite the battery of hi-tech scans and probes to which the Iceman was subjected – it was almost a decade before somebody spotted a small flint arrowhead in his left shoulder. This had sliced through an artery, causing massive bleeding which led to his death. And it was some time later that another scan found a deep cut to the right eye, from either a fall or a blow to the head, which would also have caused heavy bleeding and may have contributed to his death. This illustrates a basic and important archaeological rule of thumb – i.e. fresh analyses can often bring startling new evidence. One should never be satisfied with an existing scenario – true scientists constantly question and return to their earlier conclusions, to check them again. But very few do so.

KNOSSOS

This palace in Crete of the second millennium BC was excavated from 1900 to 1905 by the tiny but very wealthy British archaeologist Sir Arthur Evans, who named the civilisation responsible after the legendary King Minos (as immortalised in the phrase 'it is a small thing but Minoan'). The huge storage jars at the site are called pithoi and are thought to have had multiple uses, including coffins. The site is now a must for tourists, but bears a resemblance to a kind of archaeological Disneyland for its garish and highly speculative and imaginative reconstructions of architectural features and wall paintings – the frescoes at the site and in Heraklion Museum, including the famous 'bull leaping' scene, are based on tiny fragments of originals, and therefore tell one far more about the taste of the modern artists than that of the Minoans.

HADRIAN'S WALL

Britain's best-known Roman monument is the coast-to-coast wall which was begun in AD 122 to divide the Roman empire from the barbarians to the north. One would hope that, once it was built, the commander did not decide that it also needed pointing. One of the most popular tourist sites along it is Housesteads fort, with its communal toilet. To the south is the fort of Vindolanda, where a freak set of circumstances has led to the survival of hundreds of wooden writing tablets with ink script still on them. These give an amazing and amusing glimpse of army life on the Roman empire's frontier – e.g. "I have sent you…woollen socks…two pairs of sandals and two pairs of underpants" and "the lads have no beer, please send some." This last message could equally apply to some of the diggers…

ANGKOR

Located in Cambodia, this is reckoned to be the world's biggest religious monument, and comprises numerous temples extending over a vast area. The main ones are usually swamped by the almost two million visitors per year. Angkor Wat and Angkor Thom are the best-known sites, the latter famous for its impressive face towers, while both contain hundreds of carvings of charming apsaras (celestial dancers). Bluffers can display their knowledge by waxing lyrical about the depictions of 'the Churning of the Sea of Milk', a Hindu myth which some may find cheesy. The temple of Ta Prohm used to be most popular for the amazing fig-tree roots that wrap around its masonry, but is now more notorious because Angelina Jolie ran around the place in *Lara Croft: Tomb Raider*. The really accomplished bluffer will dismiss such plebeian aspects, and instead recommend the hilltop of Kbal Spean, perhaps the only site in the world where rock art is carved in running water – including lots of lingams and yonis. If you need to explain what those are, try to do so politely.

PETRA

This ancient site in Jordan was immortalised by Dean John Burgon in his famous poem 'Petra' as 'a rose-red city half as old as time', although bluffers can point out that it is every other shade of red but not that one. Some visitors actually believe that its greatest monument, the amazing rock-carved tomb entrance known as the 'Treasury', is a set constructed for *Indiana Jones and the Last Crusade*. The first Westerner known to have visited (in 1812) was a Swiss called Jean-Louis Burckhardt, and he had to learn fluent Arabic and disguise himself as a Muslim to get there, because foreigners were deeply mistrusted; even at Petra his guide accused him of being an infidel who intended to rob the site of treasure. He had to sacrifice a goat at 'Aaron's Tomb' to prove that this was the real reason for his visit. Fortunately, this is no longer a requirement for tourists.

POMPEII

The most famous Roman site in the world, its archaeological fame subsequently expanded by movies and TV series, this city was buried by an eruption of Mount Vesuvius in AD 79. Consequently its streets, houses and shops survive to a large extent, making this a truly evocative place to visit. Centuries of excavation have yielded countless works of art (statuary, mosaics, wall paintings) as well as foodstuffs. The most poignant remains are the Pompeiians who died in the eruption – encased in ash, their bodies left cavities which archaeologists have been able to fill with plaster, thus creating statue-like versions of the deceased. It has been said that the city's prison was found to contain the bodies of several hardened criminals. Pompeii's other great claim to fame is the bawdy graffiti, the countless phallic images, and of course the brothels with their paintings of the pleasures on offer, and their stone beds which suggest that not a great deal of pleasure was involved for the workers. The accomplished bluffer can always display superior knowledge by declaring that nearby Herculaneum is a far more interesting site.

FAMOUS ARCHAEOLOGISTS

As very few archaeologists have ever become world famous, you will only need to know the basics about a select short list.

If stuck, simply make up some names, the more implausible the better: in recent decades there have been archaeologists called Glob, Plog, Prat, Clot and Frankenstein. And there are so many archaeologists in the world that nobody can have heard of them all. When in a tight corner, you can escape in a single bound by citing recent work by some 'eminent' fictitious name from an obscure part of the world such as Paraguay, Albania or the University of Bradford. Do not, however, try a common name: there have been umpteen eminent Clark(e)s and Smiths in archaeology, and you may be asked to specify which one you mean.

NABONIDUS

The first known archaeologist was Nabonidus, the last king of Babylon. In the 6th century BC he and his daughter Princess Ennigaldi-Nanna dug (or rather got their minions to dig) beneath buildings and located the foundations of more ancient structures. Since archaeology as such did not then exist the average Babylonian must have thought them completely potty – but then royalty can get away with anything.

HEINRICH SCHLIEMANN (1822-90)

Schliemann is the only 19th-century archaeologist that most people have ever heard of, and he wasn't a professional archaeologist but a businessman. It is said that when he was eight his father, a poor German pastor, gave him a book for Christmas which contained a picture of Troy in flames. Heinrich became obsessed with this image, and vowed that he would find Homer's Troy one day (this underlines the dangers of exposing impressionable young minds to images of violence).

Having amassed one fortune in Russia and another in America, he retired at the age of 46 – a neat trick if you can manage it – to Anatolia (the competent bluffer will never say Turkey), looked around for a likely mound in a setting that fitted Homer's description, dug into it, and uncovered an ancient ruined town. He kept on digging and found a whole series of ancient towns, one on top of the next, until he reached the one he believed was Homer's. This feat gave rise to the adage 'If at first you don't succeed, Troy, Troy again'.

He also claimed to have discovered a hoard of gold objects in the site, and is said to have smuggled it through the Turkish customs by hiding it under the voluminous skirts of his beautiful Greek wife. It is unlikely that this would be a safe hiding place today.

Opinions are still divided about whether Schliemann should be considered a pioneer of archaeology or simply a crude treasure-hunter, especially as he dug right through the layer he was looking for. Be sure to adopt the opposite view to your opponent's.

BOUCHER DE PERTHES (1788-1868)

A minor customs official, this Frenchman pioneered the collection and identification of early stone tools, and believed they were made by humans in a remote age. Most of his contemporaries thought he was a crank, and he stated that 'I observe a smile on the face of those to whom I speak.' This is still an occupational hazard in archaeology.

Boucher de Perthes made the fundamental error, copied by many excavators since, of paying his workers by the find. With a touching innocence he offered a large reward to the workman who first unearthed human remains in his sites. Not surprisingly the prize was claimed very quickly, and even less surprisingly the jawbone proved to be a fake.

GENERAL PITT-RIVERS (1827-1900)

The well-informed bluffer should know that this early pioneer's real name was Augustus Lane Fox. While a professional soldier, he came into a big inheritance, including large chunks of Dorset, on condition that he changed his name to Pitt-Rivers. He readily agreed to these terms, as the new name was no sillier than the old. A great eccentric, he compelled his tenants to attend brass band concerts in his park on Sunday afternoons, and tried to acclimatise yaks and llamas to an English habitat.

His digs were run with precision and discipline, like military exercises. This tradition was continued later by Mortimer Wheeler (see page 108), another military man; a number of modern excavators still try to run their digs like little corporals.

SIR FLINDERS PETRIE (1853-1942)

Petrie is a towering figure in Egyptology, through the number and quality of his excavations. Unlike most of his predecessors and contemporaries he insisted on the importance of recovering all material from a site. He is also the subject of a number of famous anecdotes – for example, on returning to a site he would assess the canned foods left there at the end of the previous season. If these did not explode when thrown against a wall, he knew that their contents were still edible. Working in 19th-century Egyptian field conditions, Petrie was clearly a tough customer, as shown by his practice of using potsherds as toilet paper (one hopes he used burnished pottery rather than coarse ware). And, most famously, he sometimes wore flesh-coloured combinations because, from a distance, they made him look naked, and this helped keep unwanted Victorian lady-tourists from disturbing his work. After death, his head was placed, not in a petri dish as one might expect, but in a glass jar!

HOWARD CARTER (1874-1939)

Carter is famous because he found the tomb of Tutankhamun. After shifting 200,000 tons of sand and rock and finding nothing in six seasons of work, he deserved a little luck. The bluffer will counter talk of the treasures, or reminiscences of the London exhibition, with a disparaging attitude, referring to the vulgarity of an obsession with gold, and the unhealthy emphasis on glamour rather than information about the lives of ordinary ancient Egyptians. The really accomplished will claim to prefer the simpler aesthetic appeal of the later (and comparatively unknown) gold funerary mask of the pharaoh Psusennes to that of King Tut.

HENRI BREUIL (1877-1961)

A French priest, Breuil came to dominate the whole field of prehistory for decades, especially the subject of Ice Age cave art. During his long life he reckoned he had spent about 700 days inside the caves, copying the art, so it is little wonder that he developed vision problems. Breuil became so eminent that he was known as the 'Pope of prehistory', and many archaeologists, including Breuil himself unfortunately, came to believe he was infallible. One lifelong friend dared to disagree with him about something and was never spoken to again.

Despite his profession, it was Breuil who unleashed an obsession with interpreting all kinds of motifs in Ice Age art as vulvas. And in one bizarre episode towards the end of his life, he became utterly obsessed by a small painting in a rock shelter in Namibia which, for some reason, he believed to depict a white woman of Cretan or Egyptian origin. This 'White Lady of the Brandberg' became, thanks to Breuil, the most famous image in that country, and remains one of the best-known pieces of rock art in the world, even though it is clear that the figure is not white, and not a woman – it is a Bushman with an infibulated penis.

SIR MORTIMER WHEELER (1890-1976)

An exemplary digger who tackled big sites, 'Rik' (as he was known to his friends) preferred those with a military slant, like the great British hillfort of Maiden Castle with its enormous defences and its war cemetery. He is best known to the public as star panellist of the BBC's *Animal, Vegetable, Mineral?* in the 1950s, a TV quiz show in which three archaeologists identified objects. He was also a consummate bluffer, winning odd questions on *AVM* by previously swotting up the catalogue of the chosen museum or checking which objects had been removed from display.

Wheeler was also known as 'Flash Harry', and his wit, charisma, moustache, curved pipe and roguish charm not only appealed to the TV audience: he was an inveterate womaniser far into old age. No female digger was safe, and it is said that the 'Wheeler method' of excavation which he devised – a grid of squares and baulks – provided him with the perfect pretext for looking down into the cleavages of female volunteers and assessing their potential. After his death, a woman who had been his secretary in India recalled in a radio interview that he was the only man she'd ever met who could undo her bra while driving a Land Rover down a dirt road at top speed. Is there no end to the skills to which an archaeologist should aspire?

VERE GORDON CHILDE (1892-1957)

The most important prehistorian of the 20th century, this eccentric Australian spent most of his career as professor of archaeology in Edinburgh and then director of London's Institute of Archaeology. Although he carried out some notable excavations, most famously at Skara Brae in the Orkneys, he was best known for his syntheses of European prehistory, presented in many hugely important books which hardly anyone now reads. He was probably the only scholar who could read and understand numerous European languages and make sense of their archaeological literature! A committed socialist, he also introduced the concepts of 'archaeological culture', 'Neolithic revolution' and 'urban revolution' to the subject. On retirement he returned to Australia and committed suicide. Ironically the tiny and inconspicuous grave of this titanic scholar, in Sydney's Northern Suburbs Memorial Gardens, is located very close to the grandiose monument to Michael Hutchence, a very different kind of Australian who also committed suicide.

GLYN DANIEL (1914-86)

The foremost historian of archaeology, and an expert on megalithic monuments, Daniel was better known to the public as a populariser of the subject, and as the gastronome who wrote *The Hungry Archaeologist in France*. The personification of avuncular TV chairmen (complete with glasses and spotty bow tie), he was a leading exponent of the 'archaeology as fun' approach.

THE LEAKEYS

There are few dynasties of archaeologists, and this one starred Louis Leakey (1903–72), the founder of the 'firm' who struck it rich in East Africa's Rift Valley where ancient tools and bones were found in great quantities, his wife Mary (1913–96), who continued their pioneering work at Olduvai Gorge and other sites (a couple known affectionately as 'Bones and Stones' because of their respective specialities), and their son Richard who made some important finds, e.g., the skull named 1470 (some 2.8 million years old), despite attempts by rivals to overtake him with fossils that had cuter names like 'Lucy' and 'The First Family'. The saga continues to this day through Richard's wife Meave and their daughter Louise who are keeping the firm going.

INDIANA JONES

Probably the best-known archaeologist in the world today is a fictional professor of the discipline played by the laconic Hollywood actor Harrison Ford. Although most professionals feign to scoff at 'Indie's' adventures, and criticise the films for perpetuating the myth of the archaeologist as a romantic treasure-hunter on the trail of buried gold and lost civilisations, this is all bluff.

Secretly they welcome any portion of the Indiana Jones mystique that rubs off on them, knowing that the very word 'archaeologist' now conjures up images of Indie, with a stunning lady in tow, fearlessly overcoming insuperable odds in exotic locations. In departments of archaeology at American universities it is not unusual to find, hanging on the back of office doors, a bullwhip and a battered fedora. For a while during the 1980s it was undeniably fashionable to be an archaeologist, and learning institutions around the world were deluged with applications from aspiring Indies keen to immerse themselves in three years of archaeological studies. Little did they know about the limited career prospects, and grindingly dull hours of research, but it didn't matter. Professors of archaeology were perceived as adventurous, exciting, resourceful and – most importantly – cool.

𝕭

'The image of the archaeologist – rightly or wrongly, but mostly rightly – is that of an eccentric, humourless bore: one need only recall the British magazine **Private Eye***'s repeated descriptions of a "man with beard in hole. . ."* '

ARCHAEOLOGY ON SCREEN

As anyone who hangs around with them knows, archaeologists are a pretty boring crowd on the whole. This is why the wit and repartee of the Mortimer Wheeler/Glyn Daniel double-act, 30 years before the Indie films screened, were a refreshing revelation to the British public on BBC Television's *Animal, Vegetable, Mineral?* It's worth remembering that these unlikely household names were, respectively, the BBC's first and second 'TV Personality of the Year'. How many archaeologists have held that title since then?

To the public, the image of the archaeologist – rightly or wrongly, but mostly rightly – is that of an eccentric, humourless bore: one need only recall the British magazine *Private Eye*'s repeated descriptions of a 'man with beard in hole', or the *Two Ronnies* joke that 'for sports fans there will be rugby with Eddie Waring, boxing with Eddie Tiring and archaeology with Eddie Downright-Boring'.

It is also worth remembering that in the very first episode of BBC Television's sitcom *Hi-de-Hi!* about a dismal holiday camp of the 1950s, the newly appointed entertainments manager, Jeffrey Fairbrother (played by the suitably po-faced Simon Cadell), was supposed to be a Professor of Archaeology at Cambridge who had decided on a change of job because his wife had said he was far too boring.

No reference to archaeologists in comedy, however brief, would be complete without mentioning the British film *Carry on Behind* (1975) which begins with the brilliant Kenneth Williams, as 'the distinguished archaeologist Professor Roland Crump', delivering a talk entitled 'Getting to the bottom of things', oblivious to the fact that a wrongly supplied film of a stripper, projected behind him, is turning his innocent account of an excavation into a torrent of filthy double-entendres.

Youngsters were given a different version of the supposedly exciting world of archaeology by the three 'Mummy' movies starring Brendan Fraser as an Indiana Jones-type swashbuckling adventurer. *The Mummy* (1999) and *The Mummy Returns* (2001) both had Egyptian settings, while the sequel *The Mummy: Tomb of the Dragon Emperor* (2008) moved the action to China and brought the Terracotta Army (see page 92) to life. Unfortunately, and in stark contrast, a movie of 2017, also called *The Mummy*, starring Tom Cruise as a 'soldier of fortune who plunders ancient sites for timeless artifacts and sells them to the highest bidder', was not well received by the public, with one critic declaring sourly that 'it should have been kept under wraps'.

If you take the view that Glyn Daniel's 'archaeology as fun' was easily the sanest attitude to the subject on TV, you need to be wary of decrying subsequent developments – the belief of those who make today's television documentaries that secrets, mysteries, treasures, dead bodies, and computerised and dramatised reconstructions are all but compulsory – together with endless repetitions after commercial breaks. Above all, these shows must pretend that the presenters are on a longed-for personal quest, instead of just trying to make good money, earn some airmiles and become TV personalities.

'These TV documentaries have become a tired and reductive format, filled with clichés satirised by the BBC's wonderful Philomena Cunk as "shouting at helicopters" and "starting sentences in one place... and finishing them in another".'

It is vital that the presenter must adopt a gimmick, such as standing dramatically on a windswept clifftop or riding a bike; tossing Lorna Doone hair while wearing a Belstaff oilskin jacket; sporting a Tintin quiff while wielding a machete; wearing leggings and trendy trainers; wearing black and using an umbrella in full Egyptian heat; or sporting red-dyed hair and an excruciating accent.

It is equally indispensable that the presenter must walk in and out of shot, delivering killer soundbites, preferably looking back over their shoulder. Each statement needs to be an assertion, as they stride purposefully off camera. This has been called the 'walk of shame' for academics who are desperate for the book sales offered by TV.

The cynical bluffer will declare that, in many cases, less effort seems to have been put into the script than into booking the airline ticket. Overall, these TV documentaries – which often stretch what might have made an interesting half hour into an interminable and repetitive 60 or 90 minutes – have become a tired and reductive format, filled with clichés satirised by the BBC's wonderful Philomena Cunk as 'shouting at helicopters' and 'starting sentences in one place... and finishing them in another'.

As all archaeologists know, real archaeology is often like watching paint dry – nothing much happens, and it happens very slowly. This means that it's difficult not to concede the necessity for TV companies to bring in presenters who dash about with the frenzy of fleeing Pompeians to infuse archaeology with a sense of dramatic urgency. While recommending a measured approach to their epic speculations, the bluffer could speculate that after *The Naked Archaeologist* and *Extreme Archaeology*, can a series of *I'm an archaeologist, get me out of here* be far behind in this general dumbing-down?

Well, no, as it happens. Early in 2015 a British TV channel ran a ten-part series called *10,000 BC* in which 20 volunteer men and women were transported to a wilderness in Bulgaria and expected to live for two months like Stone Age folks by hunting and foraging for food – despite their total lack of relevant skills or knowledge. It is hard to imagine what the point of this futile exercise was, other than to appeal to the baser instincts of viewers who presumably were hoping for some sex, violence, gore, etc. It was described as a 'social experiment re-creating conditions of the Stone Age', but its contribution to archaeology was non-existent.

One recent phenomenon in Britain is that some of the TV presenters have been head-hunted by universities and appointed as 'professors of the public understanding of history' or suchlike – doubtless with a hefty salary – which means that basically they have been given a chair in 'being a TV celebrity'. The sad aspect of such appointments is that, in these times of crisis and cutbacks, many real archaeological academics have been laid off. We are living in the Irony Age.

Another modern tool that has been seized upon is the drone – a toy that is basically an expensive and fun new way to drop your camera.

BRAVE NEW WORLD

In the 30 years since this book was first published, archaeology has altered immeasurably – not least in terms of its practitioners: the subject has become more humdrum and anonymous. The big personalities, the remarkable and dazzling characters of the past, are long gone and it is highly improbable that we will ever see their like again.

But of course the greatest revolution has occurred in the techniques available – the magical new technology, from computers to satellites, from all kinds of scans to genetic analysis. However, as the bluffer can knowingly point out, just because everything is different doesn't mean that anything has changed. And in fact, there can be such over-reliance on the new whiz-bang gadgets that their eager users may lose the plot…

Indeed, there is no longer any need for archaeologists to do much of anything, as they can get machines to perform so many tasks for them – they no longer need to fly or swim as aerial photos are now taken by satellites, and underwater exploration is done by unmanned robot vessels. In fact, excavation is now the last bastion of human archaeologists, but doubtless the day is not far off when that too will be undertaken by mindless automatons (though some might say that this has been going on for a long time).

Archaeologists now routinely employ GPS (known as Geeks Play with Satellites), a useful method for those who have not yet had the time or the training to learn to read maps. They are the kind of people who visit foreign places but constantly use their phone to find their way around without actually looking to see what is around them.

Google Earth and other collections of satellite photos (many of them a remnant of the Cold War) are a godsend to the Google Geeks and Satellite Sallies who love to gaze at photos and try to find endless supposedly unknown archaeological features and sites, some of which may even prove eventually to exist! They are also, of course, a means of being able to work on regions which are totally inaccessible because of warfare or impenetrable vegetation. It would be a brave archaeologist indeed who preferred to enter Syria or Afghanistan rather than study their archaeology on a computer screen in the comfort and security of one's armchair.

Another modern tool that has been seized upon is the drone – a toy that is basically an expensive and fun new way to drop your camera. Drones – little remote-controlled helicopters with a camera that can take aerial shots for you – are well named, because they are often operated by drones of a different kind. And of course many archaeologists have been droning on and on for years, both in lectures and in print.

And now you have the opportunity and the expertise to join the ranks of the droners.

GLOSSARY

Activity area Scatter of artifacts where archaeologists like to imagine that something happened.

Artifact Any object that looks as if people made or used it.

BP 'Before the Present'. As archaeologists tend to live in the past, their 'Present' is actually 1950.

Barrow A tumulus.

Culture Archaeological term for regional groups of similar artifacts, often equated with different peoples. Also that which grows on mugs and plates in the excavation hut.

Dating methods Courtship rituals adopted by archaeologists who want to share digs.

Early/Late The first/second part of a period. A popular alternative system is Lower/Middle/Upper. Archaeologists love to divide periods, phases and cultures into handy chunks like this, with the lines drawn through gaps in the evidence.

Gender archaeology Feminist archaeology.

Hypocaust A floor under which hot air circulates and heats the room above. The meeting place of any symposium of archaeologists constitutes the perfect example.

Hypothesis A guess.

Lecturer One who talks in someone else's sleep.

Lifeway Awful American term meaning 'way of life', as in 'prehistoric lifeways', but tolerable in comparison with the unspeakable 'prehistoric foodways'.

Living floor Floor on which archaeologists think people lived.

Magdalenian A period at the end of the Ice Age, nothing to do with the *Da Vinci Code*.

Mastaba Flat-topped type of Egyptian tomb for high-ranking officials and priests, the butt of many jokes which ensures that students remember it.

Megalith A big stone.

Microlith A little stone.

Midden An accumulated heap of trash (UK); a glove without fingers (US).

Neanderthal Early human type that derives its name from bones found in the 19th century in the Neander Tal (valley) in West Germany. Bluffers can reveal that the valley itself was named after a German hymn-writer called Neumann who pretentiously gave his name the Greek form of Neander (new man).

Necropolis An area of tombs; a kind of city set apart for the dead, something like Cheltenham.

New Archaeology (or rather, Archeology, since it was largely perpetrated by Americans) – Old Archaeology dressed up with jargon (e.g., 'Middle Range Theory' and the 'Hypothetico-Deductive Method'), and presented with a fair degree of pomposity.

Palaeolithic The first and longest period of prehistory, named after the Greek for 'old stone' (Palaeo-lithos).

It is followed by the Neolithic (new stone) age, and in-between, inevitably, is the Mesolithic (middle stone) age. Each of them is further subdivided into phases (see Early) and cultures, mostly named after sites.

Posthole Any hole too small to be a storage pit.

Post-processual or **Interpretive archaeology** Anything Goes. In interpreting the past, even the opinions of idiots, charlatans and sci-fi writers have to be considered as valid as your own.

Ritual All-purpose explanation used where nothing else comes to mind.

Rock art Nothing to do with album covers, but anything drawn, painted, carved or engraved on rock.

Speleology The study of caves. Good chance of encountering troglodytes.

Spoilheap Mound of discarded dirt resulting from an excavation, probably so called because it spoils the view.

Storage pit Any hole too big to be a posthole.

Stratigraphy The different layers encountered in a site, one above the other. In general, given a pair of layers, the upper one is younger than the one that lies beneath.

Theoretical archaeology Last resort of the desperate and illiterate.

Theory A series of hypotheses.

Tumulus A barrow.

Typology The arrangement of tools, pottery, etc, into different categories according to shape, size, date or function. It takes an unbearably tidy and organised mind to enjoy this kind of thing: Pitt-Rivers was a master of classification and German archaeologists revel in it.

AUTHOR'S POSTSCRIPT

In academic circles, archaeologists and humour were not bedfellows until fairly recently. The great pioneer was undoubtedly Glyn Daniel whose many years of gossipy, jokey editorials in the journal *Antiquity* (1958–86) still shine out; the volume of the 'Best of' these editorials is a pleasure to dip into, while Glyn's autobiography, *Some Small Harvest* (1986), contains some hilarious anecdotes.

When I studied 'Arch, and Anth.' at Cambridge more than 40 years ago, there was precious little humour around. Inserting humour into archaeological writings occurred sporadically; apart from Glyn's work, one should mention a study by Warwick Bray (1981) concerning humour and cartoons in archaeology. Across the Atlantic, Kent Flannery soon established himself as the arch-exponent. In France, François Bordes had a great sense of humour, as did his draughtsman Pierre Laurent whose cartoon book *Heureuse Préhistoire* (1965) was, and remains, outstanding. From the early 1970s onward the practice of writing serious papers with jokey titles spread rapidly in the English-speaking archaeological world, though not elsewhere: in France, for example, only Bordes comes to mind even now as having tried this with his *'Savez-vous remonter les cailloux à la mode de chez nous?'* (1980). Elsewhere it remained taboo – indeed one Spanish archaeology professor published a paper that denounced the practice. On the other hand, Australia's late arrival on the archaeological scene ensured that it had no such hang-ups, and *Australian Archaeology* (est. 1974) is always one of the liveliest and most humorous of journals.

Where contributions by non-archaeologists are concerned, Gary Larson's *Far Side* cartoons have been pre-eminent, deservedly enjoying worldwide popularity; but Laurent's above-mentioned pioneering contribution to the genre should not be overlooked, nor Gonick's *Cartoon History of the Universe* (1990), nor the fact that Bill Tidy, Mike Williams and others in Britain have long maintained production of great cartoons on archaeological themes.

This was the state of play when, in 1988, the first *Bluffer's Guide to Archaeology* was published. There were strict ground rules – fixed length, no illustrations, and a semi-factual/semi-humorous style – which made the task a little daunting. But the major problem was lack of a precedent. Perhaps the nearest thing, albeit completely different, was Philip Rahtz's *Invitation to Archaeology* (1985), although the influence of the writings of Glyn Daniel, Kent Flannery, and Paul Courbin's hilarious *What is Archaeology?* (1988) need to be acknowledged.

Initially it was never imagined that the audience for the book was likely to extend much beyond academic circles in the UK. But soon tales reached me of pirate

Xeroxes circulating everywhere; German professors wrote to Bluffer's to say how their enjoyment of it proved their nation has a sense of humour; France's top archaeological bureaucrat translated it into French; and in Harvard one day a graduate student rushed up and told me I was a cult (at least I think that's what he said).

I was pleased but bewildered by these reactions which simply prove that one should always write for oneself, as it's impossible to know what others will find amusing.

One incidental but amusing aspect of the book was that very few of the people who appeared in it seem to have recognised themselves (though everyone else recognised them), while many people who fear they are in it are not. One friend told me that all my subsequent work – after this unexpected hit – would be an anti-climax, which was a depressing thought.

When I first began to jot down notes for the book, I ran through the gamut (very short as gamuts go) of jokes about archaeology. First, there was Agatha Christie's famous *bon-mot* about an archaeologist being the best possible husband because the older his wife gets, the more interested he is in her.

There was some further material with potential, such as Spike Milligan's old gag (in *There's a Lot of it About*) that 'In Mexico, archaeologists believe they've found the lost city of Tecotuhuatahicatihaci. They're having great difficulty in digging it up and even greater difficulty in saying it.'

The Two Ronnies also included a few suitable jokes in their regular 'news items': 'The teeth of a prehistoric mammoth were found today in Sussex, a double event according to archaeologists: not only are they the world's oldest teeth but they were found in the world's largest glass of water'; 'An Oxford university professor has returned from the Middle East with the Dead Sea scrolls. However, it's clearing up nicely, and he'll be back at work on Monday.' And finally, with their legendary subtlety, they also told of the disappointed archaeologist who crossed Nefertiti with Titicaca and got two sets of Nefercacas…

Unfortunately, it was only after the book was published that I learned that in South American archaeology – where the old 'hu' and 'c' spellings have been changed to 'w' and 'k' (e.g. Tiahuanaco is now Tiwanaku) – the literature now abounds in references to a people called the 'Wankas' – a name of amazing aptness in a discipline like archaeology.

There are countless examples of archaeological bluffing around us, especially in print or online where much chest-beating goes on. Humourless theory and writing continue to proliferate from the same cast of bores, and rocketing careers are still being founded on aggression, pretentiousness, dishonesty and downright sloppy work. People are building reputations and achieving recognition (among colleagues and in the media) although the data they use are hopelessly wrong and distorted (never let facts get in the way of a good story). Bluffing, in short, flourishes as never before.

It is when archaeology takes itself too seriously, and when archaeologists become self-righteous about their mission in life, that the balloon of pomposity needs bursting. It's time to blow some more raspberries.

Paul Bahn.

A BIT MORE BLUFFING...